THE PAST IN PERSPECTIVE

Series Editors: *C.C. Eldridge and Ralph A. Griffiths*

REVOLUTION IN RELIGION

THE PAST IN PERSPECTIVE

Series Editors: *C.C. Eldridge and Ralph A. Griffiths*

C.C. Eldridge is Reader in History at St David's University College, Lampeter, University of Wales.

Ralph A. Griffiths is Professor of Medieval History at University College of Swansea, University of Wales.

Other titles in this series:

THE PAST IN PERSPECTIVE

REVOLUTION IN RELIGION

THE ENGLISH REFORMATION, 1530–1570

David Loades

CARDIFF
UNIVERSITY OF WALES PRESS
1992

© David Loades, 1992

British Library Cataloguing-in-Publication Data
A catalogue record for this book is available from the British Library.

ISBN 0-7083-1141-5

Typeset by Alden Multimedia Ltd., Northampton
Printed in Great Britain by Billings Book Plan Ltd., Worcester

Contents

To Judith, who also prepared

the index

Editors' Foreword

Each volume in this series, *The Past in Perspective*, deals with a major theme of British, European or World history. The aim of the series is to engage the interest of all for whom knowledge of the riches of the world's historical experience is a delight, and in particular to meet the needs of students of history in universities and colleges – and at comparatively modest cost.

Each theme is tackled at sufficient length and in sufficient depth to allow each writer both to advance our understanding of the subject in the light of the most recent research, and to place his or her approach in due perspective. Accordingly, each volume contains a historiographical chapter which assesses how interpretations of its theme have developed, and have been criticized, endorsed, modified or discarded. Each volume, too, includes a section of substantial excerpts from key original sources: this reflects the importance of allowing the reader to come to his or her own conclusions about differing interpretations, and also the greater accessibility nowadays of original sources in print. Furthermore, in each volume there is a detailed bibliography which not only underpins the writer's own account and analysis, but also enables the reader to pursue the theme, or particular aspects of it, to even greater depth; the explosion of historical writing in the twentieth century makes such guidance invaluable. By these perspectives, taken together, each volume is an up-to-date, authoritative and substantial exploration of themes, ancient, medieval and modern, of British, European, American and World significance, after more than a century of the study and teaching of history.

C.C. Eldridge and Ralph A. Griffiths

Explanatory note

References in the course of the text to the Bibliography at the end of are indicated by a bold number in round brackets (**3**).

References to the Illustrative Documents which follow the main text are indicated by a bold roman numeral preceded by the word 'DOCUMENT', all within square brackets [**DOCUMENT XII**].

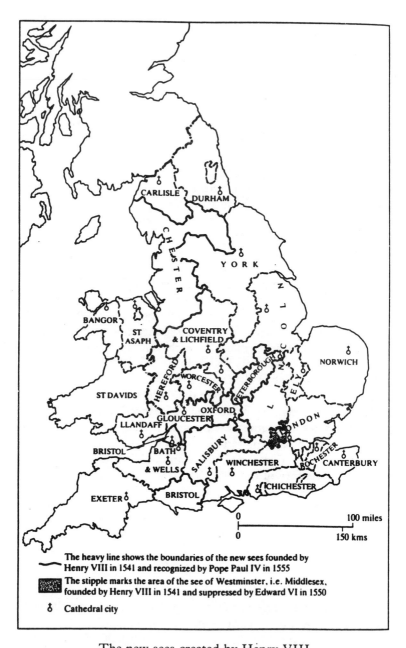

The new sees created by Henry VIII.
(Reproduced from *The Emergence of a Nation State, 1529–1660*, by A.G.R. Smith, by permission of Longman)

1. The Interpretation of the English Reformation

Until a few years ago, the history of the English Reformation was written either by the heirs of the victors or by the heirs of the vanquished. The predominant tradition might be broadly described as Whiggish, celebrating the success of protestantism as a victory for progress, both intellectual and constitutional. This tradition ran from John Bale (*The Image of Both Churches*, 1545) and John Foxe (*Acts and Monuments*, 1563, 1570) in the mid-sixteenth century, via Thomas Fuller (*Church History of Britain*, 1655) in the mid-seventeenth to John Strype (*Ecclesiastical Memorials*, 1720) in the early eighteenth. It was renewed and revitalized in the early nineteenth century by the controversy over catholic emancipation and by the Tractarian movement, which produced the massive editorial labours of the Parker Society (active 1840–60). There were two new and learned editions of Foxe's *Acts and Monuments* in the mid-nineteenth century, one by Josiah Pratt and the other by S.R. Cattley and George Townsend. At the same time the main historical argument was maintained by J.A. Froude and J.R. Green, and became enshrined in the textbooks of the early public secondary schools in the manner satirized by Sellers and Yeatman in *1066 and All That*: '. . . Mary's reign was, however, a Bad Thing, since England is bound to be C. of E., so all the executions were wasted.' The protestant Reformation had become, by way of Queen Elizabeth's Tilbury speech and the black legend of Bloody Mary, a part of the pre-history of England's imperial greatness, a theme which continued to dominate the history curriculum down to the Second World War. The alternative tradition, which originated in the fierce polemic of Nicholas Sander's *Rise and Growth of the Anglican Schism*, became in time both apologetic and nostalgic. Association with Spain under Mary, Elizabeth and James I, and with France under Charles II and James II, destroyed the credentials of catholicism as a religion for patriotic Englishmen, a fact which most English catholics both regretted and resented. They counter-attacked as best they could,

particularly against the 'vandalism' of the destruction of the monasteries, but the eighteenth-century Church history by 'Charles Dodd'
(Hugh Tootel) and the early nineteenth-century work of John
Lingard had little appeal outside the catholic community itself. It was
not until the work of Cardinal Gasquet later in the century that the
alternative view of the Reformation began to be taken seriously by the
educated community at large. It is always difficult for any religious or
ideological group to account satisfactorily for prolonged failure. The
English protestants could cope with their brief eclipse under Mary,
describing it both as a punishment for their sins and as a trying or
testing of the Elect for eventual triumph. But the catholics could find
no such positive consolation, and for them the Reformation in
England remained an *Historia Calamitatum* until the issues largely
faded away in the present century.

Among recent historians of the Reformation, the heir to the
Anglican tradition is A.G. Dickens. In his main book *The English
Reformation* (1964) and in innumerable articles (**15, 16**) Dickens has
argued that protestantism was well established in England before
1547, building naturally upon the foundations laid by the Lollards.
Using will formulas and other testamentary evidence, he has discovered protestants as far apart as Exeter and Newcastle-upon-Tyne
in the later years of Henry VIII's reign. According to his interpretation, although the king's policies may not have been generally
popular, they attracted a substantial level of support in all sections of
society. That support was mainly, but by no means exclusively, in the
south and east of England. Hostility to the clergy and to clerical
pretensions was a significant factor, particularly among the gentry and
the townsmen, but positive factors such as the effects of humanist
education, the desire for an English Bible, and the attractiveness of
the protestant doctrine of justification all played an important part.
Responding to criticisms of his views in the second edition of *The
English Reformation*, Dickens has effectively reasserted his position,
using further evidence of a similar nature. (**15**) Other historians who
either follow Dickens or argue along similar lines include Claire
Cross, J.F. Davies and J.W. Martin. When Dickens's book first
appeared, the most recent, and by far the most thorough, work on the
subject had been published by two learned and moderate heirs of the
catholic tradition, Fr. Philip Hughes and Dom David Knowles.
Neither Hughes nor Knowles denied the reality of anticlericalism, or
the level of protestant support, but Hughes in particular argued that
the late medieval Church was by no means as black as it had been

painted, and both placed their emphasis where the catholic tradition had always placed it, upon the actions of the government, and particularly of Henry VIII. (**18, 38**)

Since the 1960s, however, a third tradition has emerged, which its protagonists call 'revisionist', but which might equally be called 'neo-catholic'. Here the main thesis is one of continuity. Not only was the catholic Church popular, fulfilling most of the spiritual needs of the people, but the anticlericalism of the period is largely a myth, a *post hoc* justification for attacks which had nothing to do with popular religion. Like the earlier catholics, the revisionists emphasize most strongly the actions of the government, but in their case that of Elizabeth rather than Henry VIII. Henry VIII and Edward VI created precedents, one for the royal supremacy and the other for a protestant establishment, but both would have been abortive without the long reign of Elizabeth. It was Elizabeth, not Henry or Edward, who converted England to protestantism. Before 1558 popular support for the Reformation was negligible, largely confined to the artisans of London, and the Lollards were no more than an eccentric fringe group, which would have been of no importance at all without the political upheavals of the mid-sixteenth century. Moreover, English catholicism was by no means a lost cause, even after a decade of Elizabeth's reign. Its roots were still strongly in the soil, and it failed eventually because its so-called rescuers, the seminary priests from Douai, neglected the main popular tradition and instead concentrated on instilling the new theology of the Continental Counter-Reformation into a sympathetic section of the educated gentry. The main protagonists of revisionism are Christopher Haigh and J.J. Scarisbrick, although Patrick Collinson, the immensely learned and authoritative historian of Elizabethan puritanism, has also lent a measure of support. (**90, 17, 22, 13**) Like most theses of its type, this revisionism has attracted a great deal of interest and sympathy, not least because it is directed against what was previously the dominant orthodoxy of Reformation scholarship. Its main weakness, like that of the catholic tradition before it, is that it postulates a very high level of power and effectiveness in Tudor government. Could any sixteenth-century government carry out so revolutionary a programme, in the teeth of both popular and aristocratic opposition, without a large measure of support in the community? And if everybody was so happy with the traditional Church, where did that support come from?

When these questions are asked, the argument can quickly become bogged down. Wills are no longer regarded as being necessarily a good guide to a testator's personal beliefs, and much 'anticlericalism' can be shown to have had its roots in personal or property disputes which had nothing to do with one party's spiritual status. On the other hand, recent research, such as that of Anne Hudson and Margaret Aston, has tended to emphasize rather than undermine the importance of Lollardy in shaping popular attitudes during the Reformation. Endless examples can be (and have been) cited from all over the country to demonstrate the continued popularity of traditional religious practices up to, during, and even after the Reformation. Susan Brigden's work on London probably goes as far as the evidence will ever permit in analysing the religious composition of that populous and powerful city (51) — showing that both traditional and evangelical views commanded strong support. There seems to be little doubt that, on a broad quantitative level, the revisionists are right. Both hostility to the traditional Church and positive enthusiasm for Protestant ideas were confined to a small proportion of the population before 1559. However, the question is not a quantitative one, but qualitative. In a democratic polity a vociferous and highly committed minority can often carry an issue against majority opinion if the majority is lukewarm and poorly organized. Sixteenth-century England was not a democratic polity, and the same dynamics do not apply, but the reformers, first humanist and then protestant, gained control of the royal supremacy which Henry VIII created for his own purposes. It scarcely mattered that both were small minorities. They were numerous enough where it signified — at court, in Parliament and in the city of London — to be able to use that control effectively. Nor were they resolutely opposed. Partly out of loyalty to the king, and partly out of self-interest, those who might have formed an effective conservative opposition failed to do so, leaving the committed catholics, such as Fisher and More, isolated and vulnerable. There was opposition, but it was uneasy in conscience and confused in aim, due partly to the fact that the leaders did not see themselves as rebels, and professed loyalty to the king. Given the kind of society that Tudor England was, there is no need to postulate a powerful movement of grass-roots dissent against the traditional Church in order to explain the Reformation. What does need to be explained is why there was so little positive and forceful enthusiasm for the catholic faith, either among the people or the aristocracy.

Great shrines which had been venerated for centuries were destroyed in a few weeks on the king's orders. There was plenty of unhappiness and grumbling, but no resistance — an instructive contrast with the fate of Henry's attempt to levy an 'Amicable Grant' in 1525. Chantries embodying the piety of generations, high and low alike, went down amidst plenty of murmuring, but no action. When a chance to return to the traditional ways was offered by Mary, it was grasped with widespread rejoicing, but the attempt to defend that situation after Mary's death was limited to the bishops and a handful of tough-minded clergy. In fact, the conservative preferences of the great majority of the people of England were almost totally irrelevant to the political action which brought the Reformation about. The weakness of English catholicism lay not in its lack of popular appeal, but in the shortage of highly committed leadership. By 1570, when that commitment did begin to appear, it was too late to recover the lost ground. The traditional Anglican thesis took such a lack for granted, and explained it partly by the abuses of the late medieval Church, and partly by the rival attractions of committed protestantism. We now know that both those explanations were overstated. The traditional catholic thesis did not accept that there was such a lack of commitment, and explained the outcome in terms of the victory of worldliness and political power. Unfortunately, the revisionist thesis does not really explain it either. By concentrating on the popularity of catholic practices, and the slight development of popular protestantism before 1559, it comes close to the earlier catholic conclusion by a different route. But we now know enough about the workings of Tudor government to know that the Crown did not have the resources (or probably the will) to defeat widespread and highly committed opposition among the English aristocracy. The Reformation succeeded both because it was promoted by the Crown, and because no such opposition appeared. Perhaps there is no single explanation for such a fact, and the reader may be able to arrive at his, or her, own conclusions from the pages which follow.

2. The Royal Supremacy, Which Made It All Possible

a) The Henrician supremacy: political and jurisdictional implications

The royal supremacy, as it was progressively established through a series of statutes between 1532 and 1536, was primarily a positive statement: '. . . the king's Majesty justly and rightfully is and oweth to be the Supreme Head of the Church of England, and so is recognised by the clergy of this realm in their Convocations . . .' [DOCUMENT I, i] The king may have been motivated originally by his desire to escape from one particular aspect of papal jurisdiction, but by 1536 he had become convinced (or had convinced himself) that God had always intended his Church to be run in such a fashion. Consequently, the statutes did not claim to create the supremacy, but merely to insist upon its recognition after a lapse of time. This was both legally and psychologically necessary. No one had ever claimed that a statute could alter the law of God, and both popular custom and humanist education encouraged the veneration of antiquity. In order to make any change acceptable, it had to be represented as a return to the good and ancient ways. Unfortunately for Henry, and even more for the principal architect of the statutes, Thomas Cromwell, in the case of ecclesiastical jurisdiction this was a transparent fiction. No one knew how to define this supposedly ancient authority, and the political bones frequently showed through the legal skin.

Henry had started originally, before there was any question of the legality of his first marriage, with two objectives. One was to secure from the Pope a title to match the *Rex Christianissimus* (Most Christian King) of the king of France or the *Rex Catholicus* (Catholic King) of the king of Spain. The second was to remove the stigma (purely formal, but real enough to a man of Henry's sensitive vanity) of being a vassal of the Holy See. This was a matter which was occasionally cast in English teeth by Continental jurists, and one over which the king had the wholehearted support of all those of his subjects who were learned enough to be aware of it. The matter of the title was resolved by academic rather than political means. Henry prided himself upon both his learning and his orthodoxy, and the rise of the Lutheran heresy gave him an opportunity to demonstrate them. *Assertio Septem Sacramentorum* (*Defence of the Seven Sacraments*) may not have been entirely his own work, but in October 1521 it earned him the resounding designation *Fidei Defensor* (Defender of the Faith), and honour was satisfied in that direction. The issue of papal suzerainty remained, and clouded the increasingly muddy water of the king's 'Great Matter' after 1527. The evolution of Henry's state of mind lies outside the scope of this brief discussion, but by the beginning of that year he firmly believed that his eighteen-year marriage to Catherine of Aragon was contrary to the law of God as set out in the Book of Leviticus. His urgent need for a male heir, the embarrassment of being married to a resident Imperial ambassador, and his increasing fascination with Anne Boleyn all contributed to that conviction, but it would be a mistake to assume that the king was being either cynical or hypocritical in his protestations. Unfortunately for him, Catherine was defending not only her honour and the status of their daughter Mary, but an equally genuine conviction that their marriage had been brought about by specific divine intervention. Conscience is a worse enemy to compromise than either pride or political self-interest; Catherine would give no ground, and Henry would brook no refusal. In other circumstances, a worldly and political Pope would probably have accepted the king's shaky canonical case, however sceptical he might have been about his motives, but in 1527 Clement VII did not have that option. The Emperor Charles V was Catherine's nephew. His power in Rome would have been great in any case, and by December 1527 the accidents of war had made it invincible.

By 1530 Henry had effectively exhausted the resources of diplomacy, although it would be another two years before he finally acknowledged the fact, and he had begun to seek an alternative to a papally sanctioned annulment. Before his fall in 1529 Cardinal Wolsey had warned Clement that his jurisdiction in England was at risk, but the harrassed Pope could not afford to take him seriously. The king had in his hands a range of arguments produced by specialist advisers such as Edward Foxe and Thomas Cranmer, which varied from restricting the Pope's authority to questions of heresy to denying it totally on scriptural and historical grounds. How convinced Henry himself was by such arguments at this stage is unclear, but he began to issue vague threats, which were misunderstood by recipients and spectators alike. It was at first assumed that the king of England was making another tiresome assault upon papal suzerainty in order to strengthen his hand; even contemporary developments in Germany had not given adequate warning that a good catholic prince like Henry might be contemplating an assault upon the Pope's spiritual jurisdiction. The king's next problem was to turn threats into action when they failed to have any effect. His first step was to browbeat the English clergy, first selected victims and then the whole bodies of both Convocations, using ridiculous charges based upon the late fourteenth-century statutes of praemunire (penalizing the clergy for exercising their jurisdiction without the king's consent), which had been left behind as relics of a previous Anglo-papal contretemps. This worked, up to a point. The Convocations bought a pardon for their non-existent offences, but refused to accept any suggestion that the king might hold spiritual jurisdiction. For the time being he did not insist, but the clergy (most of whose leaders were royal servants) had shown themselves to be vulnerable. In 1532 he returned to the charge with an orchestrated petition from the lower house of Parliament against clerical abuses. This time, in spite of some resistance, the Convocations bought another pardon by conceding a major point of principle. They agreed to submit all their future legislation, or canons, for the king's approval, and thus secured a temporary immunity from further lay attacks by surrendering their jurisdictional autonomy.

This submission was followed by the Act in Restraint of Annates (1532), which threatened to cut off the main source of papal revenue, and the Act in Restraint of Appeals, which actually severed the normal jurisdictional links (1533). So far the apparent emphasis had been mainly negative — upon the destruction of the 'usurped' power of the Pope — but the real effect was positive: to place in the hands of the king an authority which neither he nor any of his predecessors had possessed before. This reality gradually appeared through the Act for Dispensations, the Act of Supremacy, and the Act for First Fruits and Tenths (all 1534). By the time that the final Act Against the Authority of the Bishop of Rome reached the statute book in 1536, the king had absorbed most of the powers previously exercised by the Holy See. He was the highest court of appeal in ecclesiastical causes; he appointed bishops by the fiction of the *congé d'élire* (the king's licence to elect); he collected ecclesiastical taxation, and conducted visitations. (3) [DOCUMENT I, ii] However, not all ecclesiastical power resided in the king. Henry never claimed to perform spiritual functions in his own person; he was not a bishop. Nor did he ever claim the right to deprive a canonically appointed bishop of his see, although he later forced Latimer and Shaxton into resignation, and executed John Fisher. On the other hand, he and his advisers, both clerical and lay, made sweeping changes to the Church's calendar, introduced the English Bible, dissolved the monasteries (which had been an important part of the country's religious life for centuries), and twice redefined certain areas of doctrine to suit themselves (*The Institution of a Christian Man* — the Bishops' Book — of 1537; *A Necessary Doctrine and Erudition* — the King's Book — of 1543). In 1545 Henry confidently declared in Parliament that if any of his good subjects were aware of false doctrine being taught in the realm, they should 'come and declare the same to us or to one of our council'.

By 1536 the position of the English Crown could be described as Caesaro-papist, but in truth it was idiosyncratic, and highly personal to Henry. The king continued to profess himself a devout catholic, and to burn heretics. It is perhaps hardly surprising that many of those who might have opposed, and even frustrated, his policy failed to take his pretensions seriously. Was this strange 'supremacy' anything more than an elaborate pretext to get rid of Catherine? The sceptics included Pope Paul III, who offered to reopen negotiations once both Catherine and Anne Boleyn were dead. Henry may have been tempted by the offer, but he had gained too much to retreat easily. Traditional limitations upon royal authority had been breached wide open, and common lawyers such as Christopher St German wondered audibly whether the defences of the law had not been turned. However, by the time that it had become clear to the political nation that the king intended not only to hang on to his gains but to justify them on the highest principles, it had also become clear that there were substantial gains to be made by his subjects also. As the monasteries went down, and their property seeped out through the Court of Augmentations into private hands, Henry became increasingly a patriot king with the interests of the realm at heart. The nobility and gentry of England, although not without many individual qualms, had become doubly his accomplices: firstly in enforcing the supremacy in Parliament, and secondly in sharing the spoils. It remained to be seen what price they would eventually exact for their co-operation.

b) The Edwardian supremacy: the Church as a department of state

Henry VIII's death in January 1547 resulted in the succession of his nine-year-old son Edward. There were well-established precedents for the conduct of the government during a minority, but none of them included the exercise of the royal supremacy. This was particularly important because the power struggles which had gone on in the Privy Council and the Privy Chamber during the last months of Henry's life had produced a Regency Council with a markedly evangelical religious tone. The Pope, the Emperor and the King of France all awaited with interest the consequences of the old king's departure. Would the new governors of England follow the obvious dictates of political pragmatism, or would they endeavour to retain the status quo? Charles V even toyed with the idea of applying pressure by refusing to recognize the legitimacy of the new king, on the grounds that he had been born while the realm was in schism, and no valid marriages could be celebrated. However, it soon became apparent that the English Council was not going to follow either of the reasonably safe courses open to it. Within a few days of coming to power, it had taken the sensible step of appointing a single executive head, and had chosen the king's maternal uncle, Edward Seymour, Earl of Hertford. With Seymour's active encouragement, the Archbishop of Canterbury, Thomas Cranmer, then sought a fresh commission for himself from the new king, and encouraged his fellow bishops to do the same. The implications of this seemingly minor step were far-reaching. Instead of seeking to end the fourteen-year schism, the new Lord Protector was intent upon making the Church even more obviously dependent upon the Crown. Henry's bishops may have been appointed by the king, but as Stephen Gardiner, the conservative Bishop of Winchester, pointed out, it had never been denied that they were 'Ordinaries' — that is, that their spiritual authority derived from their consecration by their fellow bishops. However, it was being denied in 1547, and no amount of indignant protest could alter the fact. This significant development was followed up in July 1547 when Cranmer issued a set of Homilies, or model sermons, one of which introduced the protestant doctrine of justification by faith alone. [DOCUMENT V, i; see also below, p. 39] There was another outcry from the conservatives who pointed out, quite correctly, that this was a breach of the Act of Six Articles of 1539, which had insisted upon the traditional teaching. [DOCUMENT I, iii]

Although they had not acted with precipitate haste, Edward VI's governors had soon made it clear that they believed themselves to have the full right to exercise the royal supremacy in the king's name, as they would any other aspect of his authority. Nor was that right effectively challenged. Even Stephen Gardiner, who was deeply unhappy with the course which events were taking and did his best to defend the Henrician settlement, admitted that the king's authority was not impaired by his minority, and that his place was taken by the Lord Protector. Nevertheless, the royal supremacy had been conceived for an adult king. There was no such thing as a papal minority, and consequently no precedent for a Supreme Head who was scarcely out of the nursery. On the other hand, whether he liked it or not, Henry's supremacy had never been entirely personal. In order to have the legal armoury to enforce his will, he had resorted to Parliament, and the whole establishment had been given a statutory form, including the doctrinal statements of the Act of Six Articles. It was therefore natural that the Lord Protector should resort to Parliament at the end of 1547 in order to alter that establishment. The Act of Six Articles was repealed, ordination was permitted to married men, and the clergy were instructed to administer the cup to the laity in communion. For those of an evangelical persuasion, Parliament was merely carrying on the good work of bringing the positive law closer to the law of God. Those who were less sympathetic found themselves facing the uncomfortable fact that an authority which they acknowledged to be lawful was enjoining a religious stance which they believed to be heretical. [**DOCUMENT II, v**] The only conservative not to be troubled by this contradiction was the Princess Mary. Since surrendering to her father in 1536 she had never questioned the royal supremacy, and did not do so now. She merely asserted that her father's settlement had embodied an absolute truth, which no mere Parliament had any right to touch. Consequently she would obey her brother when he came of age, and in the mean time would refuse to be bound by any statute of which she did not approve. Her status as heir to the throne and the diplomatic support of her cousin Emperor Charles V could have made this subversive attitude extremely dangerous. Fortunately for the minority governments, and for Mary herself, it was not publicly shared by any other person of substance, and could consequently be contained, although not without trouble and embarrassment.

In spite of this lone voice of radical dissent, the role of Parliament in the supremacy became progressively greater as the reign developed. In 1549 a complete new English liturgy — the *First Book of Common Prayer* — was imposed upon the clergy by statute without reference to Convocation [**DOCUMENT I, iv**]; clergy were allowed to marry, and all ecclesiastical courts were instructed to conduct their business in the king's name. The chantries went the same way as the monasteries, only this time specifically as places of 'error and superstition'. Images and altars were removed from churches, and in 1552 a second — much more explicitly protestant — Prayer Book was authorized. On this occasion the laity were penalized for failing to attend the new services. Parliament was also significant for what it did not do. Thomas Cranmer and some of his colleagues spent a great deal of time and effort producing a new code of canon law suitable for a protestant church under royal control. But Edward's second mentor, John Dudley, Duke of Northumberland, who had overthrown the Protector in 1549, would not allow it to be presented for ratification, apparently on the grounds that it gave the reformed Church too much autonomy. This point was rubbed in, perhaps unintentionally, when another statute, designed to enlist the power of the state in preserving ecclesiastical discipline, referred such purely religious matters as the enforcement of the Lenten fast to the jurisdiction of the justices of the peace.

By the time that he died in July 1553 (still a minor), it had become clear that Edward was an enthusiastic, not to say bigoted, protestant. How much a dawning awareness of this fact affected the exercise of the supremacy by either the Protector or the Council is hard to say. His convictions may simply have been a reflection of theirs. What is clear, however, is that the circumstances in which the supremacy had been converted to protestantism were to have important long-term consequences. On the one hand, it had become institutionalized, and on the other, the inherent tension between the authority of scripture and an Erastian establishment had been effectively concealed.

c) The Marian supremacy

Mary secured her succession to the throne after her brother's death by defeating an attempted coup in favour of her cousin, Lady Jane Dudley (née Grey). This coup had been organized, with Edward's full connivance and support, by the Duke of Northumberland, Lady Jane's father-in-law. Whatever Northumberland's real motives may have been, his action was represented at the time as an attempt to preserve the reformed Church of England. It is not surprising, therefore, that Mary regarded her victory as an endorsement of her own conservative religious position. 'Right heirs for to displace I did detest,' wrote the protestant Sir Nicholas Throgmorton in explaining his failure to support Jane, and Mary's success is usually attributed to 'legitimism'. The word, however, needs to be used with caution. Some undoubtedly supported her because they believed her to be Henry's only surviving legitimate child, but she was also the lawful heir in another sense which nearly all Englishmen could accept. She had been named to succeed, in default of heirs of Edward's body, both by the last Succession Act of 1544, and also by Henry's will which that act had authorized. Consequently Mary was not entitled to deduce from the fact that her subjects endorsed her claim to the throne that they also repudiated the annulment of her mother's marriage and the supremacy legislation by which that had been achieved.

In August 1553 the new queen's conservative religious views were well known. At considerable risk to herself, she had championed the mass and the traditional rites of the Church throughout her brother's reign, and few expected the protestant settlement of 1552 to survive. [DOCUMENT I, v] However, there was also a hidden agenda. At what point Mary decided to repudiate the royal supremacy altogether, we do not know. She had given no hint of papist convictions since 1536, not even during her last and traumatic conflict with Edward's Council in 1551, but by the time that she started meeting foreign envoys as queen, her mind was made up. It was a logical decision, but an unexpected one, and one fraught with political difficulties. Her earliest confidant, the Imperial ambassador, Simon Renard, was publicly delighted but privately appalled at the risks involved. Stephen Gardiner, now Lord Chancellor, was fully supportive but realistic about the methods which would have to be used. Only Cardinal Reginald Pole, far off in Viterbo in Italy, was unreservedly delighted, and urged her to press ahead with all speed.

To his intense frustration and dismay, Mary yielded to the counsels of caution. Gian Francesco Commendone, an envoy who visited her secretly from Pope Julius III, found her zealous but determined to proceed circumspectly, and urged his master to accept that decision gracefully. In fact, Renard greatly overestimated the political strength of the protestants, but he was much nearer the mark in pointing out that many conservatives had no enthusiasm for papal jurisdiction either — especially those who had purchased land formerly in the possession of the monasteries. Moreover, the ambassador had a hidden agenda of his own — instructions from the Emperor Charles V to negotiate a marriage between Mary and his only legitimate son, Philip of Spain. In proposing this match, Charles was in fact exploiting Mary's long-standing dependence on his advice and support in order to secure a strategic advantage for Philip in the Netherlands. The queen accepted it as a genuine expression of concern for her well-being. Renard's mission consequently required him to urge that the marriage be given higher priority than reconciliation with Rome, and Charles had his own reasons for wishing the latter to follow Philip's arrival in England rather than to precede it. He wanted his son to receive the credit for negotiating the first recovery of a major heretical state. So in spite of Pole's frustration, and the somewhat subterranean efforts of Stephen Gardiner, the end of the schism did not reach the top of the political agenda until the autumn of 1554, over twelve months after Mary's accession.

Meanwhile the queen had used her authority as Supreme Head — an authority which she rejected on principle — in order to re-establish the ecclesiastical situation of 1547. In the autumn of 1553 the Convocations reaffirmed their allegiance to the traditional doctrine of the mass, and Parliament repealed the whole body of Edwardian religious legislation. The chantries could not so easily be restored, but the protestant liturgy was withdrawn, the clergy were again required to be celibate, and the ecclesiastical courts again functioned in the names of the bishops. In March 1554 a set of royal articles enjoined the revived canonical discipline on clergy and laity alike, although the queen balked at the idea of a royal visitation to enforce them. (**5, pp. 322–9**) That task was left to the bishops. The episcopal bench was purged of protestants and fellow-travellers, and many leading figures of the previous regime, such as Thomas Cranmer, Nicholas Ridley, John Rogers and Rowland Taylor, were rounded up and imprisoned. No trials took place, because there was in Mary's eyes no proper ecclesiastical jurisdiction to authorize them, but in other respects she acted with as high a hand as ever her father had done. Deprived conservative bishops such as Cuthbert Tunstall and Stephen Gardiner were restored after the merest gesture of judicial process, and new episcopal appointments were secretly confirmed by Pole, duly appointed as papal legate but still retained in the Low Countries by the influence of the Emperor.

Once Philip was safely installed in England, serious negotiations with the papacy could commence, and he immediately assumed a leading role. The main stumbling-block, as everyone had realized for over a year, was the question of the secularized Church lands. Parliament had already made it clear in April 1554 that it would not repeal the supremacy legislation without adequate safeguards, and Pole had made it equally clear that in his view such safeguards could not be given. Fortunately for Philip (and Mary), Julius III was willing to take a different view, and instructed (rather than permitted) his legate to issue a general dispensation in return for the restoration of his jurisdiction. As a result Pole returned to England, and the second Marian Repeal Act was completed in January 1555. [DOCUMENT I, vii] Strictly speaking, this act did not revoke the supremacy, because that had not been established by statute, but merely repealed all those Henrician acts which had given the supremacy form and substance. Equally, it did not confer a legal title on those persons who held former ecclesiastical property, but merely recorded that the Pope had granted an unconditional dispensation from the canonical penalties. The legal position following the act was therefore less clear-cut than at first appears. On the one hand, those who believed in the supremacy could still see Mary in that role; and on the other hand 'the possessioners' (as Pole significantly called them) could not feel free from pressure, and even spiritual blackmail, to surrender their gains.

In the formal sense, the royal supremacy disappeared with this statute, but in practice some of the substance remained. [DOCUMENT I, vi] Although the Cardinal Legate was responsible for conducting the religious persecution which soon became the most notorious feature of the reign, most of the drive came from the queen herself and from Philip, who supported her fully on this issue. Mary used her own authority to establish commissions of investigation and to control the press. The Privy Council put pressure on justices of the peace, not merely to support the ecclesiastical authorities, but also to take initiatives themselves in seeking out heretics and bringing them to justice. At the same time, some more radical protestants, particularly those who had fled to Aarau or Geneva where the reformed discipline was fully established, were abandoning the royal supremacy as they witnessed the inhibiting effect which it could have upon ideological resistance. In 1558 Christopher Goodman declared in *How Superior Powers Ought to be Obeyed* that jurisdiction must depend upon sound doctrine, rather than the other way round. Although some people, including Mary herself, believed that she was acting in accordance with the law of God in restoring the traditional order, constitutionally the catholic Church in England from 1555 to

1559 was the Church by law established, and for that reason commanded widespread acceptance from many who did not in fact support it.

Not only did Mary fail to lay the ghost of the royal supremacy but in one important sense she gave it additional substance. Before 1553, it was quite possible to argue that the successive religious statutes of Henry VIII and Edward had progressed steadily towards a superior revelation of the law of God — in other words, that Parliament was merely acting as an agency of Higher Authority. Once Mary had succumbed to sound political logic and repealed her father's and her brother's acts instead of ignoring them, it was no longer possible to argue from either side that Parliament was acting *ultra vires* (beyond its power) in legislating for the Church. It had become an accepted principle that the religion of England was the proper concern of the Crown, Lords and Commons, and not merely of the Convocations.

d) The Elizabethan supremacy: stability achieved

Elizabeth had conformed, although with some visible reluctance, to her sister's religious settlement. Mary had not trusted the sincerity of that conformity, partly because of her intense personal antipathy to a woman she always thought of as 'the little bastard', and partly because of the simple logic of Elizabeth's birth and upbringing. In this case Mary's instinct had been accurate, but it would be wrong to suppose that the new Queen Elizabeth had given any active encouragement to those protestants who were heralding her as 'Deborah' within a few days of her accession. It was the logic of their own position which caused them to pin their hopes on her, and it was her political instinct which caused her to respond. The English protestant tradition had been moulded by the royal supremacy, and had survived the years of exile and adversity by maintaining 'the face of an English Church' in Frankfurt, Strasbourg and Zurich. In spite of Christopher Goodman and the Genevan 'lobby', most English protestants continued to think in terms of an establishment, and if their faith caused them to believe that the Lord had removed Jezebel as an expression of His mercy to the Elect, then that same faith prompted them to hail Elizabeth as the agent of that mercy. She responded, partly because her own faith was of the reformed persuasion, but more importantly because it was in her interest to do so. Elizabeth hated Mary as cordially as the late queen had hated her. She also realized that her predecessor had made a critical mistake in appearing to be too favourable to foreign interests and jurisdictions. Her subjects were predominantly conservative in their religious tastes, but they had no love for the Pope, the Spaniards or the French. For both reasons Elizabeth wished to distance herself from her sister's policies as quickly and as emphatically as was consistent with basic prudence.

When Mary died, England was at war with France and in alliance with Spain, but Philip's decision to abide by his original marriage treaty, and not to press any claim to the English Crown, solved one half of Elizabeth's problem. There need no longer be any Spanish influence in England which she was not willing to admit. The papal jurisdiction, on the other hand, presented a difficult question. Given the strength of conservative religious feeling, the tense international situation, and the rival claim of Mary, Queen of Scots, Elizabeth might well have refrained from provoking papal hostility. Instead, she clearly regarded the restoration of the royal supremacy as a *sine qua non*. All her personal priorities pointed in that direction. It was remarked at the time that she 'gloried' in her father and his achievements — perhaps because Mary had been so much her mother's daughter. Also the official allegiance to the Pope was weak, not least because hostility between Philip and Pope Paul IV had disrupted communications almost as soon as they had been resumed. So Elizabeth set out to resurrect her father's legislation. Whether she originally intended to resurrect her brother's as well is a matter of some controversy. She must have known that the protestants formed only a small minority of her subjects, but they were vocal, influential, and most of them were strongly committed to the supremacy in the sense in which she understood it. This made a concordat natural, particularly as the bench of bishops which Elizabeth had inherited quickly made their opposition to any revival of the supremacy apparent. So the queen probably intended a protestant settlement from the start, and such an intention can certainly be read into the symbolism of her pre-coronation entry into London, during which she was presented with an English Bible, and publicly thanked God for rescuing her from 'the Lions' den'. Significantly, the House of Commons offered no resistance to either the Supremacy Bill or the Uniformity Bill, which introduced a slightly modified version of the 1552 Prayer Book. Thanks to the presence of the bishops, the Lords made great difficulties over both. In the case of the Supremacy Bill, they got very little lay support, and it passed comfortably; but the latter provoked a close contest which the queen eventually won by the dubious expedient of imprisoning two of her more vociferous ecclesiastical opponents.

So in the summer of 1559 the Edwardian supremacy was restored [**DOCUMENT I, viii**], by the same means which had first recognized it and then rescinded that recognition. Her father's more personal supremacy was not within Elizabeth's grasp, partly because of what had happened during her brother's reign, and partly because of her sex. Recognizing the strength of both learned and popular opinion on the latter subject, she adopted the more ambivalent title of 'Supreme Governor'. This was intended to make fully explicit the fact that she did not claim any episcopal or sacerdotal function in her own person, but it made very little difference to her jurisdictional authority. A similar scruple may, however, have lain behind the issuing of the first ecclesiastical commission on 19 July 1559. [**DOCUMENT I, ix**] The queen had been empowered by her Act of Supremacy to issue letters patent establishing commissions to exercise specific aspects of her ecclesiastical jurisdiction, and in due course the Ecclesiastical Commission became a permanent and powerful instrument of government. Although it was headed by the Archbishop of Canterbury, the majority of its members were laymen, and it certainly did not represent a covert means of restoring a measure of autonomy to the Church. Nevertheless, the authority which had been so unequivocally restored to the Crown was used at first with extreme caution and ambivalence. Elizabeth spent more time and effort circumventing the demands of puritan-dominated Convocations in 1563 and 1566 than she did in supporting the attempts of her bishops to uphold the law. The Royal Injunctions of 1559 were clear enough, but they were mainly concerned with enforcing the supremacy. When the Convocations produced a new set of doctrinal articles in 1563, the queen would not allow them to be ratified by Parliament. Having restored the lawfulness of clerical marriage, Elizabeth proceeded to make plain her personal aversion to the practice. The political reason for this ambivalence in the first decade of the reign is clear. She was endeavouring to build bridges to the religious conservatives, and to woo them away from papal allegiance into conformity. This policy was largely successful because, although the appeal of protestantism was limited, strong attachment to Rome was even more so. It came to an end in 1570 when the Bull *Regnans in Excelsis* excommunicated the queen and absolved her subjects from their allegiance. Thereafter, any refusal to accept the royal supremacy was potentially treasonable, as it had been in the reign of Henry VIII. The Thirty-nine Articles were ratified by

Parliament in 1571 and, although Elizabeth continued to be reluctant to interpret conservatism as Roman catholic, there could no longer be any doubt that the Church by law established was fully, and indeed aggressively, protestant. The patriotic union between Church and state had become full and explicit. Outside that union both recusants and separatists were regarded as public enemies.

3. The Church as an Institution

a) The structure of the medieval Church

The medieval Church was based upon the land. All its constituencies were territorial — dioceses, archdeaconries, deaneries and parishes — and the overwhelming majority of its clergy were supported by the income of land-rents and agricultural produce. Each of the twenty-six bishoprics into which England and Wales were divided had its episcopal patrimony which in 1535, when the survey of monastic property, called *Valor Ecclesiasticus*, was drawn up, ranged in value from £135 per annum for Bangor to over £3,000 for Winchester. Unlike Italy, where the early Church had naturally followed the urban pattern of the late Roman Empire, the English and Welsh sees were large, and often based in cathedral cities, such as Ely and Durham, which were little more than villages in social and economic terms. Even the poorest bishop had the income of a substantial gentleman, and the richest exceeded all but the wealthiest of the secular peers. They lived, and maintained their households, in the style of the feudal lords which, in a sense, they were. They held their temporalities from the Crown in return for homage and fealty, and discharged the same military obligations as other lords, although they were not expected to serve in person. In theory, a bishop was elected by the cathedral chapter of his see and confirmed by the Pope. In practice, he was usually nominated by the king, who used this extremely valuable patronage to reward the more distinguished of his clerical servants. Papal indulgence for this was purchased in a number of ways, by political favours and by occasionally allowing the Pope to reward a servant of his own in the same manner by a system known as 'Provision'. Monarchs were usually wise enough to avoid overtly scandalous appointments, and Popes were complacent because they realized that it was inevitable that kings would wish to control the deployment of such extensive resources. All the dioceses were originally royal foundations, and the proprietory relationship never entirely disappeared.

Parishes, on the other hand, mostly derived from private foundations. The churches had been built and endowed with their glebe lands by wealthy laymen between the eighth and twelfth centuries. By the late Middle Ages there were about 9,000 of them, covering the whole realm, and they had developed in a number of different ways. In some cases the advowson, or right to nominate to the benefice, still belonged to the heirs of the original founder, or other individuals to whom it had passed by purchase. In many other cases, it had passed to the diocesan bishop, or to the king, or to a religious house. In the last case the glebe land, or parish endowment, would also have been transferred, so that the monastery itself became the rector of the parish, and the cure was served by a member of the house. Such parishes were often better cared for than those in which the rector was an absentee whom the patron wished to favour. When that happened the actual parish priest, who served in the rector's place, was termed 'vicar' and was paid a fixed stipend out of the rector's income. The rector enjoyed not only the income of the glebe but also the 'great tithe' which was levied on the main product of the parish, usually grain. The 'petty tithe' of other produce belonged by custom to the resident priest, who might also be the rector or might be the vicar. By the fifteenth century, parish churches also frequently housed chantries or other foundations of special intent. The income of these foundations was separate from that of the parish, but was also derived from the rents of land or house property. The purpose of such foundations was usually to offer masses and prayers for the souls of the founder and the founder's kin; the priests who served them might, or might not, also assist in the parochial ministry. A foundation might consist of a single cantarist, or it might be a complete college of prebendaries, headed by a dean who would also be the rector of the parish. Glebe land and tithe formed an interface between the clergy and the laity, along which interests continually clashed, and litigation was frequent. It was these inevitable conflicts which produced most of the evidence interpreted by subsequent historians as 'anticlericalism'. (**17, pp. 56–74**)

Religious houses — monasteries, nunneries and later friaries — were similarly founded with landed endowments. The friars' fundamental vows of poverty kept their property to a minimum, but favoured monasteries became large and wealthy establishments. Monasteries were expressions of a very specific religious culture, which saw withdrawal from the world and dedication to worship and prayer, whether intercessory or general, as having an essential social and communal function. For centuries wealthy and anxious people bestowed land to maintain and expand such houses. And since the Church did not die, or fail of heirs, kings became concerned lest too much land should be withdrawn from circulation, and insisted upon licensing such gifts by the Statutes of Mortmain. By the fifteenth century, fashions in piety were changing. Monasteries were no longer attracting substantial new endowments, and the number of those responding to a monastic vocation never recovered from the devastation of the Black Death. The scale of the monastic establishment was more a monument to the piety of earlier generations than a necessity for present needs. Faith in the *opus dei* had weakened, and withdrawal from the world was no longer considered to be an advantage for intercession. The new chantries took over some of the functions which the monasteries had previously been expected to perform. By the reign of Henry VIII many good catholics believed that a proportion, at least, of the wealth of the monastic houses could justifiably be diverted to other spiritual purposes.

The influence of such views partly explains why Henry's two-stage programme of dissolution met with so little effective resistance. Some monks, and particularly some abbots, were principled opponents of the royal supremacy, but the vast majority took the required oaths without demur. The king's real motive was probably neither pious nor jurisdictional, but simply fiscal. Nevertheless, the disappearance of a whole traditional way of life, the discrediting of its values and the redistribution of its massive accumulation of land had a major impact, both upon lay society and upon the remainder of the Church. Six new dioceses were created, at Chester, Bristol, Gloucester, Peterborough, Oxford and Westminster; monastic cathedral chapters were refounded with secular canons, and many great ecclesiastical buildings were left to fall into ruin. At the parochial level hundreds of impropriated livings, or monastic rectories, passed first to the Crown and then to the lay purchaser of the estate. This not only led to a major revival of lay patronage in the presentation to livings, but also to the phenomenon known as lay impropriation, where the rectory itself was in lay hands [**DOCUMENT II, iv**, see below, pp. 27–31], and the vicar was no longer a substitute, but the only clerical incumbent the parish could expect. Instead of being strengthened by an injection of ex-monastic wealth, as most of the reformers had hoped, many parishes were impoverished by this process, and became less rather than more attractive to well-qualified clergy.

b) The dissolution of the monasteries

Monasteries, observed the reformer Hugh Latimer, were arguments for the existence of purgatory. Consequently, their dissolution was an argument to the contrary. Neither Stephen Gardiner nor the king himself agreed, but Latimer was making a valid point. Although intercession for the souls of founders and benefactors formed only a small part of a monk's activity, his whole way of life was based upon the possibility of compensating for natural and original sin by self-punishment and self-denial. This was a process which could not be completed in one short lifetime, and the concept of purgatory was a natural corollary. Purgatory had originated, not in the stark teaching of the New Testament, but in a humane reluctance on the part of the Church to consign the bulk of humanity to eternal damnation. The sharp division into saved and damned did not correspond to any perception of the way in which people actually behaved, and so the notion developed of souls spending the period immediately after death undergoing punishment and purification in preparation for an eventual entry into the Kingdom of Heaven. This period could be shortened and eased, not only by the specific intercessions of the living, but also by drawing upon the merit acquired by those spiritual athletes who spent their entire lives in the praise of God. This provided comfort and consolation, but it also created massive opportunities for the Church to market its specialist skills. Disgust with the abuses which this undoubtedly created played a large part in motivating Martin Luther's protest of 1517, and purgatory consequently became a major issue of the Reformation all over Europe.

With a few honourable exceptions, such as the Carthusians, the English monasteries had long since ceased to be credible as embodiments of the ascetic ideal. Their wealth, and the relative ease and security of the monastic life, had undermined their rigour, and they would hardly have been recognizable to Aelred, Abbot of Rievaulx in the twelfth century. There was little point in a relaxed house, which might even have too few inhabitants to maintain the full office, and the monasteries had long since lost their teaching functions to the universities. So the pious increasingly looked elsewhere for the model of Christian virtue, and chantries and educational foundations became increasingly popular. By the early sixteenth century many good catholics had reconsidered their priorities and acknowledged that the monasteries in their existing form were hard to defend. For those, like Thomas More, who believed intensely in the original ideal, reform was imperative and the diversion of at least a part of the existing endowment to other pious and charitable purposes entirely justified. Although the breaking of testaments was considered to be a heinous sin, such diversion was canonically feasible. Bishop Alcock of Ely (died 1500) had dissolved the decayed nunnery of St Rhadegund in Cambridge in order to found Jesus College, and Wolsey dissolved several small houses in the process of establishing Cardinal College in Oxford. Henry's original intention at the end of 1534 may have been the same. He instructed Thomas Cromwell, as his Vicegerent in Spirituals, to carry out an extensive visitation in order to discover the true state of the religious houses, and the early returns in 1535 suggest that his orders were carried out in a reasonably impartial way. However, as the year advanced the tone changed, and it seems that the visitors had been given supplementary (and probably verbal) instructions to paint as black a picture as possible. According to the Imperial ambassador Eustace Chapuys, Henry had been talking as early as 1533 about resuming grants made to the Church; but it is not clear when a policy of wholesale dissolution was decided upon.

Cromwell, who was strongly in sympathy with the reformers and encouraged their preaching, probably urged the king in that direction. But according to one account, his advice was '. . . that it should be done by little and little, not suddenly by parliament', and that it was other members of the council, particularly Thomas Audley and Richard Rich, who persuaded Henry to adopt a statutory solution. Whoever was responsible, the first Act of Suppression was passed in 1536. In spite of its exaggerated language about 'manifest sin, vicious, carnal and abominable living . . .', the preamble to this act made the valid point that houses with very small communities were less likely to have maintained a decent standard of observance than larger establishments with a higher public profile. It therefore adopted the arbitary, but not unjustifiable, expedient of dissolving all those houses with an income of less than £200 a year, and granting their property to the Crown. [DOCUMENTS II, i; II, ii] About 60 per cent of all the religious houses in England and Wales — some 500 foundations — came within the scope of this act; and although a few gained remission by special pleading, most had been visited and closed by royal commissioners within a year. For the first time the meaning of the royal supremacy was brought home to many ordinary people, and the reactions were decidedly varied, even in the same area. At Hexham, for example, the townsmen turned out in arms in an attempt to defend their abbey, while a few miles away at Tynemouth they anticipated the commissioners by sacking the house before the latter could arrive. On balance, the policy was unpopular, particularly in the north, and formed one of the grievances of the Pilgrimage of Grace in the autumn of 1536, but the only effective obstruction was local and temporary.

In theory the Act of Suppression had presented no threat to the greater houses, which were specifically praised for the good observance of their rules, and enjoined to receive all those fugitives from the lesser houses who wished to continue in their habits. The continuity of the monastic life appeared to be guaranteed. But it was not so, and over the next three years intimidation and political pressure produced a mounting tally of 'voluntary' surrenders by houses unaffected by the act. In 1539, before the process was complete, a further Act of Parliament vested all the lands of the surrendered houses in the Crown, and the Court of Augmentations was set up to administer them. Waltham Abbey, the last monastery in England, surrendered on 23 March 1540, and by then the Court of Augmentations had assumed responsibility for property with a capital value in excess of £1·5 million. Whether the King's motives were partly religious or wholly fiscal cannot be concluded from the surviving evidence, plentiful though that is, but the impact of the dissolution upon the Church was momentous. The mitred abbots disappeared from the House of Lords, leaving the bishops in a permanent and diminishing minority (for the number of secular peers was increasing). For a generation to come the ranks of collegiate and parochial clergy were increased by ex-monks who, willingly or unwillingly, had been sent out to serve in the secular ministry. And the whole notion of prayer as a way of life disappeared from the spiritual horizon.

In 1555, as a part of the understanding reached with the papacy over monastic property, the Bull *Praeclara* canonically extinguished the dissolved houses, and tidied up the legal status of their lands. This was not intended to mean that the 'possessioners' could rest with clear consciences, but it did mean that when Mary wished to revive the religious life, she had to start again. Her so-called restorations, six in number, were all new foundations and entirely endowed by the Crown. This was in spite of the fact that by then something like 70 per cent of the property which Henry had acquired had passed into the hands of others by grant or purchase. Mary's monastic initiative was half-hearted both in quantity and quality — about 100 monks, nuns and friars, and a capital endowment of about £40,000. It was also very short-lived. Within months of her death, her foundations were again in the hands of the Crown, and the majority of their inmates had retired to the Continent to live out their vocations in more congenial surroundings. The political nation had availed itself of Elizabeth's accession to banish, finally as it was to turn out, any lingering threat to the greatest acquisition of landed wealth since the Norman Conquest.

c) The parish church

The parish was the basic unit of religious life, and the church was the forum of its expression. The building itself was divided both symbolically and actually into two parts. The chancel, where the high altar was situated, was the domain of the clergy and the incumbent was responsible for its upkeep. The nave belonged to the people. [DOCUMENT II, iv] It was where they congregated to hear mass, to participate in the rites of passage, and to conduct parish business. They were also expected to pay for its maintenance. Although there are many recorded cases of neglect, on the whole such churches were objects of loving care and attention. Wealthy parishioners endowed them with painted and gilded images, particularly the rood and the patronal saint. The rebuilding of a tower or the erection of a steeple could involve the whole community in fund-raising activities lasting many years, as happened at Louth in Lincolnshire in the early years of the sixteenth century. Much of the Church's teaching was conveyed visually to a congregation which did not understand the liturgical language and which in the countryside was predominantly illiterate. City parishes might give their church a different atmosphere. A prosperous parish like St Peter Mancroft in Norwich not only ornamented its church but also filled it with the memorabilia of its merchants and officials. Here the congregation was mainly literate, and brought its missals and breviaries to follow the service or indulge in private devotion. The changing seasons of the Church's year, and its many feast and holy days, were marked by a wide variety of communal rituals: Corpus Christi Day processions, Rogation-tide processions, creeping to the cross on Good Friday, and above all receiving the consecrated host at Easter. It was in and through the parish church also that the small pieties and charities of the humble were offered. A few shillings or a best beast might be bequeathed to the parish to maintain a light in memory of the deceased, or to pay for an obit, a mass for the repose of his soul. Similarly modest sums might pay for the schooling of an orphan child, or the marriage of a poor girl. Most churches housed one or more guilds — friendly societies which provided a measure of security for the dependants of those who fell on hard times. Such fraternities were normally dedicated to the Virgin Mary or to a patron saint, and met together for worship and feasting as well as for more humdrum business. In richer churches guilds very often had their own altars, and some housed the splendid chantry chapels of the very grand.

Nor was it only the building and its fittings which attracted generosity. The old, established rituals were solemn and splendid, deserving of rich vestments and valuable altar furnishings. A well-supported church would provide vestments in all the appropriate colours of the liturgical year, richly illuminated service books, a gold or silver pax for the consecrated host, chrism spoons, vessels for holy water and other similar liturgical instruments. The competitive generosity of generations of parishioners often left churches with far more such objects than they required, but it was a common source of pride to be better furnished than the church in the next parish. All this accumulated wealth was in the care of the churchwardens, two in number, who were the business managers of parish affairs. They arranged for the upkeep of the nave and the churchyard, administered the parish charities, and presented offenders to the archdeacon's court for discipline.

By 1547 very little of this familiar structure and routine had changed. Parishes which had been in monastic hands now had royal or lay patrons, but this at first had little effect upon the life of the church, except in those places where parishes had used a part of the monastic church for their own worship. In many cases they petitioned successfully to continue their use, and sometimes ended up owning the whole building. The Ten Articles of 1536 and the Thirteen Articles of 1538 simplified the liturgical year, removing a number of traditional festivals from the calendar, and churches which had possessed attractive shrines and relics found them discredited and their wealth confiscated by the Crown. But the core of religious life, the mass in all its manifold forms, remained unchanged, and the traditional rituals and pieties continued much as before. One positive development seems to have been welcomed, although it was regarded with alarm by conservative clergy, and that was the introduction of the English Bible in 1539. It had no immediate liturgical effects, but the Bible-reading habit grew steadily and spontaneously over the following decade. Less popular at the time, although of immense benefit to historians, was the introduction of parish registers in 1538. Contemporaries believed that the recording of baptisms, marriages and burials was for taxation purposes [**DOCUMENT IV, v**]; and some, taking heed of the fate of the abbeys and the pilgrimage shrines, feared for their parish silver. At the end of Henry VIII's reign it was impossible for even the most rustic churchgoer to be unaware that changes had taken place, but the Act of Six Articles of 1539 had checked the unsettling growth of evangelical preaching, and restored a measure of confidence in the king as Defender of the Faith.

Thereafter, however, change was swiftly replaced by revolution. The Chantries Act of 1547 not only swept away the perpetual foundations, but also the religious fraternities, and all those small endowments for pious purposes which were in any way connected with intercession, or could be brought within the new and sweeping definition of superstition. For the first time the mass was seriously challenged as the central act of worship, and although the theological debate would have passed over the heads of most parishioners, the consequence in the shape of the *First Book of Common Prayer* could not be avoided. Its use was prescribed by statute in January 1549, and after Whitsun no other form of service was legal. [**DOCUMENT I, iv**] By later standards the first Prayer Book was conservative, and could, with a little ingenuity, be made to look and sound much like the traditional services. But the fact could not be long disguised that it was fundamentally different, and that it was the policy of the government to make that difference abundantly clear. Several services were diminished, or removed from the liturgy; the mass was replaced by a communion service, and the language of the whole celebration became English. The Prayer Book was widely resented and resisted, and it played a major part in stimulating the south-western rebellion of 1549, which was a widespread and dangerous movement. However, the level of resistance actually achieved fell far short of what would have been necessary to stop the protestant advance. Over the next four years the entire structure and atmosphere of parish worship changed. Images and elaborate vestments were removed by order of the Council; rood screens were dismantled, and altars replaced by communion tables. In their place came, in theory at least, a much higher level of congregational participation, and much greater emphasis on preaching. When a new and protestant form of ordination was issued in 1550, the new priest was no longer presented with the traditional sacramental instruments, the paten and chalice, but with a Bible to signify that his main function was to be the preaching of the word. In 1552 the first Prayer Book was in turn replaced with a simpler and more unequivocally protestant order, which no amount of ingenuity could make to resemble the mass. Again the use of the new order was prescribed by legislation, only this time the laity were also subjected to penalties for failing to attend their parish church — the first time that this had been done. Finally, in the same year a blow which had been long feared eventually fell. The new protestant services required much less in the form of liturgical equipment (except for bigger chalices), and royal commissions were sent out to 'take up' superfluous plate, to be melted down for the king's 'urgent causes'. By the time that Edward died in 1553, the whole of the ancient and comfortable order of parish worship had been changed, even to the appearance of the church itself, now bare of ornament, whitewashed, and adorned with the royal arms and texts of scripture. **[DOCUMENT IV, ii]**

Considering the magnitude of the revolution and the venerable nature of the customs which had been overturned, the effectiveness of the Edwardian Reformation at the parochial level was remarkable. Compliance was reluctant and far from universal, but the great majority of churchwardens and incumbents did more or less as they were ordered. It was, however, very largely a negative revolution. There were certainly more protestants in England in 1553 than there had been in 1547, but the main protagonists of change, such as Archbishop Cranmer, were the first to admit that they had not really converted the people of England to a new piety. **[DOCUMENTS IV, iii; V, iii]** That failure became apparent when Mary threw the whole machine into reverse after August 1553. The mass returned, traditional rites were resumed, and the sacraments returned to their central position in worship. The clergy were again required to be celibate, and the old service books and vestments were brought out of hiding. Much had gone beyond recall, and it was an expensive business to re-equip a church to its former standard. Even parishes which welcomed the restoration most warmly made do with painted roods and hastily retrieved altar stones. Nor were all parishes enthusiastic. The protestant message had found an echo in many places, particularly in and around London, and there was a good deal of deliberate foot-dragging. Nevertheless, on the whole the Marian regime was welcomed, and, had it continued, something very like the late

Henrician situation would have returned to parishes all over the country.

It did not continue, and by the summer of 1559 the Edwardian legislation had been re-enacted. For some years Elizabeth's government proceeded gently with the enforcement of conformity, and many catholic and quasi-catholic practices continued with a minimum of concealment. Such tolerance was political rather than principled, and rapidly disappeared after the papacy launched its offensive against the queen in 1570. However, Elizabeth lived long enough, and pursued a sufficiently consistent policy, for the settlement of 1559 to take root and to become generally perceived as 'the face of an English church'. The only thing that had not changed throughout the turbulent years of the mid century was the structure of dioceses and parishes, archdeaconries and deaneries. The church courts continued to function throughout, tithes were collected (or litigated about), and churchwardens administered the consequences of each turn of the liturgical wheel. By 1570 the parishes were if anything more important than they had ever been, because they had also started to become the basic units of secular administration, and by the end of the century churchwardens were administering the poor relief which Elizabeth had accepted the responsibility to provide by statute.

d) Cathedrals and colleges: a new role

Medieval English and Welsh cathedrals fell into two broad categories, monastic and secular. A monastic chapter consisted of the monks of the house, headed by the prior, and the endowment was the endowment of the house itself. A secular chapter consisted of a specified number of canons or prebendaries, headed by the dean. In such cases, the deanery and the prebends were separately endowed, the prebendal lands normally being associated with specific parishes, and there were also some communal endowments, not earmarked, which were used for the upkeep of the building and other general purposes under the control of the cathedral chapter. The secular cathedrals, of which the greatest was York, were not directly affected by the Henrician legislation. The Chantries Act of 1547 removed the luxuriant growth of intercessory foundations which operated within all major cathedrals, but did not touch the establishments themselves. After 1540 these were known as the cathedrals of the 'old foundation'. Like the parish churches, their functions changed with successive religious settlements, but their basic form was not altered. When the greater monasteries surrendered, eight cathedrals were converted to secular chapters — Canterbury, Rochester, Winchester, Ely, Norwich, Worcester, Durham and Carlisle. In each case the new establishment was highly conservative. The last prior became the first dean and some (but not all) of the former monks became canons. The endowment of the dissolved house was then granted to the new foundation, with an appropriate charter. In addition, six new cathedrals were established for the new dioceses founded in 1540, each housed in a former monastic church, and using the personnel and revenues of the dissolved monastery in the same way: Westminster, Gloucester, Peterborough, Chester, Oxford and Bristol. Westminster was reabsorbed into London in 1550, briefly refounded as an abbey from 1556 to 1559, and became a collegiate church after the Elizabethan settlement. Gloucester and Worcester were briefly amalgamated from 1552 to 1554, but otherwise these new foundations remained as one of the most positive legacies of Henrician policy, and their total endowments produced an income approaching £20,000 per annum — about 15 per cent of the income of all the dissolved and surrendered houses.

The rise of protestantism after 1547 produced a sustained attack on the cathedrals and their revenues. They were denounced by radical preachers as 'dens of loitering lubbers' ('abbey lubbers' having been a favourite pejorative for the monks). The thinking behind these attacks is easy to understand. Not only were many canons former monks, but the whole purpose of a cathedral establishment resembled that of a monastery — the maintenance of a constant round of daily worship, with particular emphasis upon the sacrifice of the mass, and no parochial responsibilities. Pastorally, there was very little justification for their existence. On the other hand, from the government's point of view they had a very practical use, in providing the financial support necessary for diocesan administration. The bishop's chancellor, the archdeacons and other diocesan officials were by custom provided to prebends, even when the patronage remained in the hands of the Crown, as was at first the case with all cathedrals of the 'new foundation'. Prebends also formed useful patronage for more general purposes, and the less a canon was required to reside the better. Second-rank royal officials might be rewarded with a number of such preferments, which together produced a good income and involved minimal duties. Deaneries, like bishoprics, could be similarly used at a higher level. Edward Wotton, for example, councillor and ambassador under Edward, Mary and Elizabeth, was Dean of both Canterbury and York. On the other hand, when many parochial livings were poor, particularly in towns and cities, and the quality of the rank-and-file clergy unsatisfactory, the cathedrals could be used to provide leadership and support. Minor canonries for the vicars of neighbouring parishes could make their livings significantly more attractive, and the inclusion of a few notable preachers among the resident canons could supply a desperate need, particularly in the more remote dioceses such as Durham and Carlisle. So although the radicals kept up their attacks sporadically throughout the reigns of Edward and Elizabeth, they made no impression upon government policy, and indeed some radicals accepted prebends in order to gain more scope for their preaching talents.

The restoration of traditional worship by Mary led to an Indian summer of cathedral observances. Choirs and music — an important part of the old order suppressed in the later and more puritanical days of Edward — returned with a flourish. Ordinations generally increased, and the traditions of the corporate, quasi-monastic form of life and discipline were again insisted upon. (94) [DOCUMENT II, iii] Mary used her cathedrals, as Elizabeth was to do, as spiritual power-houses, concentrating high-quality clergy in the closes, where their example could be used, it was hoped, to raise the tone of the whole diocese. Her reign was too brief for the success of this experiment to be assessable, but it certainly influenced the fortunes of the cathedrals thereafter. There was no return to Edwardian starkness. Music continued, and developed a distinctively Anglican tradition; the cathedral patronage which Mary had largely transferred from the Crown to the bishops remained to strengthen the episcopal control and to prevent the secularization of chapters which might otherwise have occurred; choir schools revived and became a part of the Elizabethan educational renaissance. The queen, who notoriously disliked married clergy, even managed to keep the closes celibate, apart from the deans themselves. All this conservatism, of course, made the puritans even more hostile, but the survival of the cathedrals is a significant example of the continuity which was one of the distinctive features of the English Reformation.

Collegiate churches, which had the same format as a cathedral but without either the status or the variety of functions, for the most part went down in 1547. The exceptions included those colleges which existed primarily for educational purposes — at Oxford and Cambridge principally, but also in some other places such as Eton and

Winchester. In spite of near-panic in both universities, the dissolution of those colleges was probably never intended. It would have
been totally at odds with the government's expressed intentions, and
although it is easy to regard such expressions with cynicism in the
light of the outcome, recent research has suggested that the reprieve
or rescue which used to be postulated was not necessary. A few other
collegiate churches survived for idiosyncratic reasons, usually specific
royal protection, like the foundation of St Catherine by the Tower or
the chapel at Windsor Castle. Westminster was even refounded on
that basis in 1559, after its second dissolution as an abbey. Such
foundations were few, and it is difficult to generalize about their
purpose. They were, in a small way, like the cathedrals, relics of the
old order embedded in the new Anglican establishment.

4. The Theological Revolution

a) The humanist attack upon materialism

Materialism afflicted the late medieval Church in two ways which were distinct but connected. The first arose from the very nature of the Church as an institution, and its integration with contemporary society. With bishops as feudal lords, abbeys as great landowners, cathedral dignitaries as royal officials, and parish priests as farmers, the material basis of the Church's activities could never be forgotten. Moreover, although that basis was supposed to be protected by the priority which was always theoretically accorded to the things of the next world, in fact constant vigilance was necessary to defend it from attack or erosion. The possession of wealth, and the attitudes of mind which that engendered, were a far cry from the original message of Christianity, and there had never been any shortage of voices raised within the Church to point that out. The orthodox defence had always been that Christ had ordained a visible church to act as a vehicle for his Holy Spirit in the world, and that independent resources were necessary to enable that ministry to be performed without constant secular interference and domination. For that reason (and for others less respectable), those teaching the doctrine of apostolic poverty had always been in danger of excommunication for heresy. The distinction between the acceptable and the unacceptable was a fine one. Francis of Assisi (died 1226) became a saint and the founder of a major religious order; Peter Waldo (dead by 1218) became a heretic, and yet many of their ideas were similar. Humanists such as Erasmus and John Colet were therefore operating within an ancient and honourable tradition when they criticized the clergy for covetousness and preoccupation with worldly affairs. **[DOCUMENT III, i]** Neither they, nor John Fisher and Thomas More who shared many of their ideals, taught the doctrine of apostolic poverty, or believed that the Church should be without resources. What concerned them was that the resources should be properly used, and should be clearly understood to be the means to an end rather than an end in themselves.

However, it was very difficult to insist on spiritual priorities without raising the issue of materialism in its second form. This arose naturally from the inevitable, and at times overwhelming, human preoccupation with salvation. For many centuries the Church had taught that both faith and good works were required, but faith had tended to get taken for granted, and attention had been focused upon good works. There confusion soon arose. If it was meritorious to feed the hungry, clothe the naked, and preach the faith to the unbeliever, was it not equally meritorious to pay someone else to do those things for you? If it was meritorious to build an altar to the glory of God, was it not even more meritorious to build a whole church? Moreover, the prayers of a hired professional could be so much more efficient — and continuous — than one's own stumbling and distracted efforts. At the same time, contrition, the secret penitence of the heart which was supposed to be the precondition for the forgiveness of sins, was so hard for an outsider, even a confessor, to evaluate — hence the symbolism of outward and visible penance. Penance was supposed to be a ritual act of humiliation, performed in person and in public, but that equally came to be commutable for a cash payment. All this meant that the search for salvation acquired the air of a market-place, perfectly reflected in the image of the recording angel keeping a ledger account for each individual sinner. Even when the unit was not cash, it tended to be material in some other sense: candles lit, pilgrimages (in the sense of physical journeys) undertaken, or rituals performed.

The humanists were not the only people to object to this debasement of spiritual values. Earlier generations of mystics and reformers, such as Richard Rolle (died 1349) and Thomas à Kempis (died 1471), had done the same. But the humanists had an intellectual edge and a fashionable appeal in high places which their immediate predecessors had lacked. This derived originally from their study of classical antiquity, the history and languages of the ancient world. In its Italian homeland, this renaissance had many pagan overtones, and its philosophy accepted the positive goodness of created matter. It led to a new sense of historical perspective, and an awareness of the value of secular education in the service of the state. But a knowledge of Greek and some awareness of the culture of the Hellenic world also produced a new alertness to the language and meaning of the New Testament. Erasmus published an edition in the original language in

1516, and urged his readers to pay more attention to the word itself than to the centuries of accumulated commentary and tradition under which it had been almost buried. (**42, 48**) The humanist message was clear: return to the values and practices of the early Church; the Christian has a direct and personal relationship with God, and does not need the elaborate jurisdictional and sacramental machinery which the Church has developed. Such views were not heretical. Erasmus disliked monastic vows, having been forced to take them himself without a vocation, but he never rejected either traditional sacramental teaching or the authority of the papacy. It was a question of emphasis and priority. An act of piety or charity was pleasing in the sight of God, but could not, and should not, be computed in some kind of statistical accumulation. Erasmus's English followers, Colet, Fisher and More, each showed the influence of the ascetic tradition more clearly than he did himself, but their emphases upon the scripture and upon the importance of education were the same.

All these men were reformers in the proper sense of the word. They wished to purge the Church of materialism, not by taking away its property or by changing its doctrine, but by bringing its clergy back to a sense of their true and original purpose. In other words, they saw the corruption of the Church as superficial, not fundamental, and in that they differed from Luther and his followers. Had Luther not thrown down his challenge in 1517, it is quite possible that the English Church would have been reformed along humanist lines, as happened with the Spanish Church under Cardinal Ximenes. Henry VIII himself had been given a good humanist education before there was any question of antagonizing the ecclesiastical authorities. He was aware of the errors of the Vulgate translation, and of the arguments in favour of vernacular scriptures, long before these became issues, and in the dispute between Luther and Erasmus over free will he was firmly on the side of the latter. In seeking clues to the apparent paradox of a king who rejected both Luther and the Pope, who defended the mass and introduced the English Bible, we should look among the teachings of the Christian humanists. [**DOCUMENT III, ii**] (43) We should also remember that there were arguments of religious principle for reducing the wealth of the Church, or at least for redistributing that wealth, and that those arguments can be found in Colet's famous sermon of 1511, in the writings of Erasmus, and in the life of John Fisher, the example of whose frugality spoke louder than any words.

b) Justification by faith alone

St Augustine of Hippo in the fifth century had taught the pre-eminent importance of faith in the process of human salvation, and when the implications of that teaching first dawned on Martin Luther in about 1515, he believed that he was merely rediscovering an ancient truth once generally accepted in the Church. [**DOCUMENT V, i**] He also believed that that truth had been abandoned, or perhaps rejected, by ecclesiastical authority because it presented insufficient opportunities to profit from human gullibility. 'The just shall live by faith', St Paul had said, and faith could only be the gift of God. It could not be worked for, or sought after by study. [**DOCUMENT V, i**] To Luther, the meaning of this came as a revelation. Intellectually he had been nurtured at the University of Erfurt in the philosophy of William of Occam (died 1347), which had simultaneously proposed the total depravity of the natural man and his full responsibility for his own destiny. Taken seriously, as Luther did take it, this was a philosophy of despair. No man could be perfect, and yet God was insisting upon something very close to perfection as the qualification for heaven. He was at the same time making man a sinner, and punishing him for being so. It was for this reason that Luther later claimed that he had come close to hating God for his injustice. He had striven, desperately and in vain, with his own sense of sinfulness. Driven from his legal studies into the order of Augustinian canons, he found no peace in what was supposed to be the most perfect form of Christian life. He was ordained priest, but still had no sense of communion with God, and he drove his confessor to distraction with his misdemeanours, real and imagined. Only when human responsibility was taken out of the intellectual equation could it be resolved. Man was indeed depraved, and in a sense responsible for his own depravity, but it did not matter because this no longer spelt damnation. So overwhelmed was Luther with the relief of this conviction that he did not notice, and never fully accepted, that he had gone beyond Augustine. The latter had indeed taught justification by faith, but not justification by faith alone, which was the necessary condition for the full sense of emancipation which Luther enjoyed.

Once seen, this liberating truth could only be proclaimed. [**DOCUMENT III, iii**] Why had it not been proclaimed before? And why, when it was proclaimed, did ecclesiastical authority not only reject it, but denounce its proclaimers as heretics? There could only be one reason: the rejection of salvation by works made a large proportion of the Church's offices redundant, and drastically reduced both the power of the clergy and their opportunities for material gain. Who would pay for masses, let alone indulgences, if such things were irrelevant to their spiritual well-being? It was simply covetousness, materialism, which in Luther's eyes motivated his condemnation. So he and his followers came to regard the traditional Church as corrupt in the same sense as a simoniac is corrupt — a fundamental poisoning of doctrine and teaching by greed. For this reason the Pope became antichrist. Not only did this ideological position lead inevitably to conflict, it also squeezed out the reforming programme of the humanists. Too many of their targets seemed to be the same, and even after Luther and Erasmus had quarrelled irretrievably over free will in 1525, many conservative ecclesiastics never understood or accepted the difference. In Spain the once well-received humanists became 'luteranos', and so remained until they had been driven out of public life. Nevertheless, the response to Luther, particularly in Germany, revealed that he had struck a loud chord of common experience. Many German towns had good reason to dislike the clergy within their walls, particularly the regulars who paid no taxes and took no share of civic duties and responsibilities, but who took substantial profits from the devotion of the faithful. The confessional was particularly resented as intrusive and as offering unrivalled opportunities for blackmail and conspiracy. Misrepresentation became endemic on both sides. Just as the Lutherans could see nothing but avarice behind the traditional sacramental system, so the Catholics could see nothing but diabolical self-conceit in its rejection. They counter-attacked with their own accusations of greed when religious endowments were converted to secular purposes, and inflated the predestinarian elements implicit in Luther's teaching to support charges of anarchism and antinomianism, that is, emancipation from all legal constraints.

Luther's ideas were familiar in some places in England almost as soon as they were published. Some of his books were certainly being read and discussed in Oxford and Cambridge by 1520, which was why Wolsey found it necessary to burn them at Paul's Cross in the same year. Nevertheless, justification by faith alone did not find the same immediate response in England as it had in Germany, and it was some time before any substantial part of his work was translated into English. This may have been because the English clergy were already more effectively under lay control than was the case in any part of politically fragmented Germany. There certainly seems to have been nothing like the fierce anticlericalism which inspired some early Lutheran woodcuts; and the confessional was not a grievance in the same way. Some early English reformers who were not 'Lutherans' in any general sense, such as William Tyndale, shared his rejection of free will, but the English were for the most part pursuing different priorities in the 1520s, and the indigenous heretical tradition, namely Lollardy, had nothing to say on the subject. It was from Switzerland rather than from Germany that predestinarian ideas took hold in England in the 1540s. Justification *sola fide* (by faith alone) was first officially advocated in Cranmer's Homily of July 1547, and was enshrined in the eleventh of the Forty-two Articles of 1553, the first complete statement of English protestant doctrine. [**DOCUMENT III, v**]

The appeal of this doctrine in England seems not to have lain primarily in emancipation from clerical oppression, which scarcely existed, but rather in the search for individual spiritual security. Naturally, those who embraced such a concept believed that they possessed the divine gift of faith. How else would they have come to such a conclusion? The possessors of faith were the elect of God, and such grace could not be lost or forfeited, because faith was not an intellectual conviction or an emotional persuasion, subject to human instability. The followers of this teaching not only believed themselves to be personally saved, they also believed that they constituted an elect congregation in the place where they were. In its most extreme form this could constitute a 'gathered' church, which acknowledged no outside authority, spiritual or temporal. In Geneva, and in Scotland which was free to follow Genevan teaching after 1560, it was expressed in the idea of a 'covenanted' church, which could embrace a whole nation. In England, on the other hand, it had to contend with the equally powerful ideology of the royal supremacy. The result was a somewhat uneasy compromise, whereby the elect were prepared to accept Elizabeth as one of themselves, and thus to acknowledge the validity of her authority, while the queen in turn accepted with reluctance their vision of England as a new Israel. The toughness of the puritan nationalism which this produced was to be one of the most enduring legacies of the English Reformation to posterity.

c) The mass

The central and principal celebration of the late medieval Church was the sacrament of the altar, normally called the mass. A sacrament was defined by St Bernard of Clairvaux (died 1153) as 'a sacred sign or a sacred mystery', an object or material of common use invested with symbolic significance. A ring presented in a certain way in certain circumstances signified the joining of two people in marriage; water, administered in a ritual cleansing, signified admission to the Church. So the offering of bread and wine in the eucharist symbolized Christ's sacrifice upon the cross, and the reception of the bread by the people symbolized their membership of the body of Christ. However, by St Bernard's time, in the twelfth century, there was already uncertainty and dispute about the relationship between the symbol and what was symbolized, particularly in the case of the eucharist. Because Christ had said at the Last Supper, 'This is my body', referring to the bread which the disciples were eating, and 'This is my blood', referring to the wine, there were those who believed that the eucharistic elements must be in some real sense that same body and blood. The prevailing view in the early Middle Ages had been that the identity was spiritual, but that did not satisfy the scholastic passion for precise definition, and Cyril of Alexandria (died 444) had long since taught that the presence was corporeal. It was only by eating the body of Christ *corporaliter* (in its material substance) that the recipient could participate in the immortality of the Saviour. This concept had strong emotional appeal, but was contrary to common sense and to normal spatial perceptions. A solution to this problem was found in the Aristotelian distinction between 'substance' and 'accident', as propounded by St Thomas Aquinas (died 1274) and others. By this theory the accidents of size, shape, colour, weight, taste and the like could be detached from the substance, which was metaphysically and not physically defined. This in turn enabled a doctrine to emerge whereby the eucharistic elements could be substantially and corporeally the body and blood of Christ, whilst continuing to look, taste and feel exactly like bread and wine. The eucharist thus became more than a sacrament in the normal sense; it became a miracle of a special kind. However, a miracle has to be occasioned, and ordinary bread and wine had to be transformed in some specific way. Some believed that this transubstantiation was brought about by the faith of those receiving the elements, but such a view left considerable room for ambiguities and imprecision. **[DOCUMENT III, iv]** (88) It was simpler and more appealing to believe that the transformation took place when the celebrant spoke the words of consecration. Such an explanation was also readily comprehensible by generations of ordinary people who had an implicit faith in magic, and accepted as a matter of course the magical effects of verbal formulae. So the eucharist became the miracle of the mass, performed by the priest for the benefit of the people.

Concentration upon the miracle wrought by the priest altered the nature of the celebration in a number of ways. The communion of the people became an ancillary feature, insisted upon only at Easter, and frequently dispensed with. At the same time, belief in the corporeal presence of Christ in the elements made the consecrated host itself an object of devotion. So high a mystery could be no mere commemoration, and it became seen instead as a veritable re-enactment of Calvary: a re-presentation of the sacrifice of Christ offered by the priest. The authority of the priest, and the distinctiveness conferred by his orders, thus became greatly enhanced, and mere attendance at mass, without any reception, became counted as a meritorious action on the part of a lay person — a contribution to the credit side of the heavenly ledger. Much of this change had come about as a result of pressure from popular conceptions (or misconceptions) and was not, in the early sixteenth century, enshrined in papal or conciliar decisions. There was still room for debate and disagreement within the limits of defined orthodoxy. Transubstantiation, for example, was not a dogma until it was defined by the Council of Trent (1545–63). Nevertheless, the mass became the heart of the quarrel between catholics and protestants, and generated passions which are now hard to comprehend, except by grasping that what was implied was more important than what was stated.

To Luther the mass was a secondary issue. He disliked transubstantiation because he disapproved of the crude materialistic manner in which it was frequently interpreted, and because of the part which it played in setting the priesthood apart from the laity. If the mass was a sacrifice, then the priesthood was a sacrificial caste. To Luther justification by faith made all believers priests, because all had direct access to God; but not all were called to the ministry of the Church. He rejected the sacrificial interpretation, and insisted on the communion of the people, but was in two minds about transubstantiation. Eventually he settled for a subtle variation of his own, which has been dubbed 'consubstantiation', whereby the corporeal body and blood were deemed to be present alongside the substance of bread and wine. It was for this reason that later catholic inquisitors insisted upon affirmation being made that, after the words of consecration, the corporeal body and blood of Christ were the only substance present in the elements, a point brought out very clearly at the trials of Cranmer and Ridley in April 1554. (**4, Vol. VI, p. 441**) Few other reformers followed Luther on this issue, most rejecting any corporeal presence whatsoever, and this remained a constant bone of contention between reformed and evangelical churches. The most extreme view, ascribed to Ulrich Zwingli of Zurich but probably not held by him, was that the eucharist was simply a commemoration of the Last Supper, and that its sacramental significance lay only in the symbolic meal. [**DOCUMENT V, ii**] The holders of this view were known as 'sacramentarians', and were considered by the orthodox to be the ultimate blasphemers. It was this heresy which stung King Francis I of France into a policy of persecution in 1534, and of which Thomas Cromwell was accused at the time of his fall. The view which was embodied in the Edwardian and Elizabethan formulas in England was that of a 'real' but spiritual presence. The whole notion of sacrifice was categorically rejected, and the emphasis was placed on commemoration and communion. The sacrifice of Christ had been made 'once for all upon the cross', and the eucharist was 'a memorial of that his precious death until his coming again'. The consecrated elements were to be treated with seemly respect, as an aspect of the public order of the Church, but no more. Thomas Cranmer was the principal architect of this Anglican view, deriving his ideas partly from early medieval writers such as Ratramus (died 868), and partly from Continental contemporaries such as Martin Bucer and Peter Martyr Vermigli. He differed sharply from Luther, but only slightly from the vastly influential John Calvin, and there were few disputes on this contentious issue among English protestants after 1552.

There were two main reasons why protestants became so exercised about the mass, and why catholics defended it with such zeal. The first was the critical role that it played in the establishment of the *potestas ordinis* (sacramental authority), and consequently of all claims to clerical and papal jurisdiction. The political implications of the priesthood of all believers were shattering for the traditional ecclesiastical establishment. The second reason was that the adoration of a consecrated host as though it were the person of Christ was seen by protestants to be idolatry in its most obvious and unjustifiable form. In sharp reaction against the materialism of late medieval worship, the protestants had resurrected the Old Testament sin of idolatry — that propensity to pay divine honours to created matter which had so frequently been the downfall of Israel. The mass was idolatrous because it confused spirit and matter. This the catholic Church denied, but it was precisely those aspects of the sacrament to which the reformers took strongest exception which were selected for formal affirmation by the Council of Trent.

d) The Word of God

The Bible had always been accepted as a foundation-stone of the Christian faith. Its authors had been inspired by God, and its books enshrined not only the history of the dealings of Jehovah with his chosen people, but also the only full and authentic record of the life and mission of Christ. However, the Bible was a very complex book, and although the medieval Church might take a simplistic view of its origins, it did not make a similar mistake over its interpretation. Although Christ had preached to the poor and ignorant, he had been operating within a religious tradition which all his hearers would have understood. His apparently simple and revolutionary message needed careful handling by a Church which had become a powerful international institution with numerous vested interests. There was also a more creditable reason for caution. Although the lessons of scripture, and particularly of the New Testament, were of eternal validity, they had actually been written down at a specific time in the past. When Christ ascended into heaven, after his resurrection, he not only left behind a visible Church — a human institution — but also the Holy Spirit, 'the Comforter', to dwell within the Church and to ensure its continuing faith. The traditions of the Church, the decisions of its councils and popes, and its developing corpus of canon law, were thus deemed to be the work of the Holy Spirit — or at least carried out with his blessing. The Church was consequently insistent that its own traditions were of equal authority with scripture when it came to matters of faith, a view clearly expressed by Edmund Bonner, Bishop of London, in his homily *Of the Nature of the Church* (1555). For both these reasons, the reading of scripture by the laity was severely discouraged and vernacular translations were frowned upon, although not actually forbidden in most parts of Europe.

In England they had been forbidden by Convocation in 1408, as a result of the rise of Lollardy. The Lollards were the followers of John Wycliffe (died 1384), an Oxford theologian who had challenged a number of orthodox views, particularly on the wealth of the Church and the authority of the clergy. His followers wanted a simpler and purer Church with a larger role for the laity, and to that end had translated the whole Bible into English. They had then extracted texts to suit their own purposes, and had circulated commentaries on them. For a few years it had seemed that Lollardy, which attracted support in high places, might become a serious threat to the English Church. But the hostility of the Lancastrian kings and the débâcle of Sir John Oldcastle's rising in 1414 finished it as a political movement. It survived strongly into the sixteenth century at a parish level in parts of the Home Counties, but its most important legacy was an awareness on both sides of the potentialities of the English Bible. It was not from any Lollard source, however, that the first printed English scripture came. Luther had translated the whole Bible into German by 1522, and William Tyndale, influenced by his example — and to some extent by his doctrine — had translated the New Testament by 1525. The first edition was printed at Worms in 1526, and imported into England in significant numbers. (**52, 103**) It made an immediate impact, and was swiftly banned, first by episcopal and then by royal authority. However, demand had been stimulated to an extent which the Lollards had never achieved, and eight different versions (some of them by other translators) had been published abroad by 1532. Thereafter, thanks partly to the king's 'Great Matter' and the consequent resignation of Sir Thomas More, the religious climate in England began to change. In 1534 the Convocations asked Henry to approve an official translation. He did not actually do so until 1537, but by then three complete Bible translations had been printed in England without hindrance, following Miles Coverdale's pioneering effort of 1535. In 1538 it was decided to accept the so-called 'Matthew Bible', mainly the work of John Rogers, as the official version, and in 1539 the clergy were instructed to provide a copy in each parish church, and to encourage the laity to read it for themselves. (**51**) After Thomas Cromwell's fall there was something of a reaction, and in 1543 an attempt was made to restrict access to the Bible, but it was short-lived. Even the restored catholic Church under Mary, which allowed grave doubts to be expressed about the propriety of vernacular scripture, did not attempt to withdraw the Great Bible, confining itself to prohibiting unauthorized preaching or dispute upon its contents. So, from 1539 onward, the English Bible became one of the most powerful formative influences on popular religion, and one of the main reasons why the traditional pieties could be phased out during Elizabeth's reign with so little overt resistance. In Wales the same effect was achieved a generation later, with a vernacular New Testament in 1567, and William Morgan's Bible in

1588. During Elizabeth's reign the most influential English Bible was probably that published in Geneva in 1559. All other versions were superseded by the Authorized Version in 1611.

Catholic objections to the 'open Bible', on the other hand, were not altogether unreasonable. Although there was nothing intrinsically heretical about vernacular scripture, it undoubtedly led to wide diversities of opinion which were hard to control, and some of which were politically and ecclesiastically disruptive. The orthodox protestant view, shared by such English divines as Nicholas Ridley and John Aylmer, was that scripture needed no 'lively expositor', containing within itself all that was necessary for salvation in a form which the ordinary Christian could comprehend. Whether or not the Bible contained everything necessary for salvation, it was palpably absurd to claim that it was self-explanatory. The protestants were driven to that position by an *a priori* need to escape from the authority of ecclesiastical tradition. Because they believed that the Church had become irredeemably corrupt, both in customs and teaching, they had to argue that the Holy Spirit no longer dwelt within it; in other words, that it was no true church. For this reason the whole tradition of commentary and exegesis, going back to the eleventh century when the corruption was alleged to have set in, was null and void. Also, having denounced the traditional clergy for the misuse of their authority, they had no desire to adopt similar pretensions themselves. In practice, of course, believing that they were the true Church, the protestant clergy in every country, including England, assumed the exegetical role themselves; but they did so with an uneasy conscience, being aware that they were compromising the principle of authority *sola scriptura* (in scripture only) which had lain close to the heart of Luther's original revolt.

At the same time, the catholic Church also impaled itself upon the horns of a dilemma. When humanist scholars had pointed out, in the middle years of the fifteenth century, that there were many errors of translation between the original Greek of the New Testament and St Jerome's Latin Vulgate, their discoveries had been welcomed. Erasmus's Greek New Testament of 1516 had also been well received; but by the time that the Council of Trent met in 1545, serious doubt had set in. Why had the Holy Spirit allowed the Church to operate for nearly a thousand years with a faulty translation of its most important book? At a time when the protestants were insisting that the Holy Spirit had not dwelt in the so-called Church, this had serious implications. So, in spite of the evidence of their own eyes, and their scholarly consciences, the fathers at Trent had to insist that there was nothing wrong with the Vulgate after all, and that it was to remain the only authorized version. Subsequent vernacular translations were consequently made from St Jerome's Bible, a circumstance which caused the protestants some amusement, and gave them a distinct advantage in controversy.

5.   The Faith of the People

a) Lollard roots

Lollardy did not begin as a popular religious movement, but as one of a number of esoteric, theological disputes within the University of Oxford. John Wycliffe, its originator, wrote in a particularly impenetrable Latin style, and although several English works were also attributed to him, it is not certain that any of them is authentic. Nevertheless, his ideas were revolutionary in a number of respects. Like Marsilius of Padua, the author of *Defensor Pacis* (*Defender of the Peace*) who had been excommunicated in 1326, shortly before Wycliffe's birth, he cast doubts on the authority of the papacy, and glorified the Godly Prince. He denounced clerical wealth, rejected transubstantiation, and restricted membership of the true Church to the Elect. He also objected to monasticism, advocated clerical marriage, and believed strongly that the scriptures should be translated and made available to the laity. This was in many respects a more radical programme than Luther's, but Wycliffe did not have Luther's impact. In spite of his known heresies, he died peacefully in his bed in 1384, and was only posthumously condemned. Printing was not invented until the 1450s, and in any case Wycliffe did not have Luther's flair for popular presentation. Instead of being set out in a series of hard-hitting pamphlets, his ideas were filtered through the sermons of a group of his disciples known as the 'poor preachers'. They gained some success and notoriety because they struck responsive chords at the court of Richard II (1377–99). The king and his Parliament were at odds with the Pope, and had recently enacted the Statutes of Provisors and Praemunire, aimed at restricting papal jurisdiction. These had culminated in the Great Statute of 1393, which was a political manifesto against Pope Boniface IX. Anticlericalism was fashionable, and the courtiers who laughed at Chaucer's friar and pardoner would have been familiar with Wycliffe's sharper criticisms. It was a group of such aristocratic supporters who in 1395 drew up the manifesto known as the 'Twelve Conclusions', which foreshadowed many of the demands made by the later reformers. This complained of the subordination of the English Church to Rome, transubstantiation, the consecration of physical objects, prayers for the dead, pilgrimages and the use of images in churches.

The circumstances of Richard's deposition, and the urgent need of Henry IV for ecclesiastical recognition and support removed any chance which these aristocratic dissenters may have had of gaining control of the machinery of power. The statute *De Heretico Comburendo* (On the Burning of Heretics) of 1401 was a serious setback, and the decision of Convocation in 1408 against vernacular scripture was another. By the time of the Oldcastle rebellion in 1414, Lollardy was already a spent force at the political level. Wycliffe's main influence was to come through the Bohemian reformer Jan Huss, who had read his works and shared many of his ideas. Huss was burned by the Council of Constance in 1417, but his death provoked a major uprising in Bohemia and resulted in the establishment of a 'Hussite' church which survived into the seventeenth century. Meanwhile, in England the Lollards (the word was originally a Low German pejorative meaning 'mumbler') had become a diffuse and unfocused popular movement. The Twelve Conclusions had not been a creed, but a set of reforming demands, and had consequently not stressed positive ideas such as vernacular scripture. There was no Lollard creed, and no central doctrine which made them distinctive and around which they rallied. The situation was also made more confused by the habit of the ecclesiastical courts, which described any eccentric or heretical belief coming to their attention as 'Lollard'. After its earliest and most active phase, the movement has been described as a state of mind rather than a sect, and that is how it should be viewed. (**33, 37, 40**)

[**DOCUMENT IV, i**] There were Lollard groups, or cells, in places like Amersham (Bucks.) which persisted for over a century, but they had no church of their own, and no organization. In spite of their fierce dislike of images, and of the 'magical' elements in popular religion, they did not, on the whole, refuse to take part in the worship of their parish churches. (**34, 40**) They were not, therefore, recusants in the later sense. They conducted their own meetings for prayer, for discussion, and above all for the clandestine reading of the English Bible, but they had no regular ministry and no defined membership. They described themselves as 'the known men', and preserved both their communications and their integrity by personal and informal networks.

After the middle of the fifteenth century, there appears to have been a decline in Lollard activity, but this may be no more than an impression created by a declining interest on the part of the ecclesiastical authorities. By the same token, the revival which seems to have taken place between 1490 and 1520 may reflect an apprehensiveness caused by the growing chorus of educated criticism. The Lollards were not educated. Some of them were clergy and some were prosperous merchants, but the majority were craftsmen or small yeomen and their families. They were not proletarian, much less rootless, and often represented the more solid and respectable elements in their communities. As heretics they were pertinacious rather than heroic. A lack of ideological commitment led to frequent recantations, but relapse was the rule rather than the exception, and those who were burned were nearly always relapsed rather than obdurate. In 1506/7 Bishop Smyth of Lincoln dealt with sixty Lollards at Amersham and twenty at Buckingham, of whom all but two recanted and did penance. In 1521 Smyth's successor, John Longland, rounded up nearly 350 suspects in the same area, and must have shattered the Lollard connection in that part of his diocese. Not only were there many more recantations and a handful of burnings, but the accused denounced each other and quarrelled among themselves in a manner which suggests that their collective morale had been destroyed. However, by the 1520s the situation was changing. A number of Buckinghamshire Lollards are known to have attended John Colet's sermon in 1511, and to have approved warmly of his reforming ideas. When William Tyndale's English New Testament became available in 1526, the Lollards were quick to appreciate its superiority to their own obsolete texts, and provided a ready market for the smugglers. By 1530 the ecclesiastical authorities were becoming increasingly confused as they faced three distinct but overlapping challenges: humanist, Lutheran and Lollard, and the labels themselves are misleading. Those who had been influenced by the new Continental ideas were made of sterner stuff than the 'known men'. Their resolution and willingness to argue back at first took the bishops by surprise [DOCUMENT IV, iv], and their numerous printed books were much harder to suppress than the Lollard manuscripts of an earlier generation, even though some of them were the same texts.

The extent of Lollard influence over the early stages of the English Reformation has been much debated, but it cannot be coincidence that the principal areas of protestant dissent in the 1540s — London, Essex and the Home Counties — were largely the same as the Lollard

areas of half a century earlier. Moreover, the early priorities of the
English protestants — vernacular scripture, the role of the Godly
Prince, the destruction of images, and the rejection of transubstantiation — were much the same as those of the older popular heresy. As
a proportion of the population as a whole the Lollards were few, and
they were not active proselytizers, but they provided a fertile soil for
ideas which might otherwise have seemed unacceptably foreign.
When John Foxe and his friends hailed John Wycliffe as 'the morning
star of the Reformation' they were endeavouring to create a protestant
historical myth, but there was a measure of truth in their claim.

b) Popular radicalism

Radicalism may be defined in many ways, but in this context the
radicals were those who did not subscribe to the idea that the visible
Church was 'permixt', that is, made up of both the elect and the
reprobate. Both catholics and mainstream protestants accepted that
the fate of the individual soul was a mystery known only to God. A
man might be convinced of his own election, but no one could know
another's destiny. The apparent quality of a person's life, his or her
ostensible diligence in faith or good works, could be no more than an
indicator. Consequently, the visible Church could be legitimately
equated with a national or international institution, and its truth could
be determined by pragmatic tests of doctrine or usage. To the catholic
these were Universality, Unity and Antiquity; to the protestant,
Preaching, Sacrament and Discipline. To the radical, on the other
hand, the visible Church consisted only of the Elect, and the Elect
were defined as those persons who, on reaching years of discretion,
had made an acceptable confession of their faith. It thus became a
fraternity of consenting adults, and could not be defined in any other
way. Neither the Roman catholic Church, nor the Church of England,
nor the reformed churches of Zurich or Geneva, were 'true' by this
criterion. The radical was thus a separatist, or sectarian, committed to
the concept of a 'gathered' church, and believing himself to have a
unique relationship with God. Because such separatists almost invari-
ably rejected infant baptism (when they did not reject baptism altogether), they were often known as 'Anabaptists', or re-baptizers, a
label which they vehemently rejected but which has stuck.

In principle John Wycliffe had been a radical, but that aspect of his
teaching did not emerge very often in the opinions expressed by later

Lollards, and their attitude was not sectarian. Every generation produced a few eccentrics, individuals who denied the divinity of Christ, or claimed that he 'took no body' of his mother; some rejected the written scriptures altogether, claiming that the Holy Spirit enlightened the Elect; others accepted the New Testament but rejected the Old. Such people were undoubtedly heretics, but cannot be classified in any other way, and their significance was slight. The origins of English sectarianism are hard to trace, because before 1547 all overtly protestant groups partook of that nature without being radical in intention. Early references to conventicles, such as that at Hughenden in Buckinghamshire in 1530, can usually be identified as Lollard meetings. John Harrydance, the Whitechapel bricklayer who preached to large congregations in his back garden between 1537 and 1539, was certainly an early example of a 'mechanic preacher', an illiterate who had learned large parts of the Bible by heart, but he was neither radical nor sectarian. His audience varied from day to day, and the only thing that Archbishop Cranmer could allege against him was preaching without a licence. The first 'gathered' congregation was probably a mixed group of Flemings and Englishmen who were discovered to have been meeting in the house of John Raulings in London in 1532. They were described as 'Anabaptists', and may have been involved in the distribution of radical literature such as the so-called *Anabaptists' Confession*, but the few hints which can be gleaned of their ideas are unremarkable.

With the establishment of protestantism as official doctrine in 1549, the picture becomes clearer. Two Anabaptists were executed by Edward's government: George Van Parris, a Dutchman, who in the English context seems to have been an individual eccentric, and Joan Bocher, an undoubted radical, who claimed that there were '1000 of her sect' in London. If she was right, their meetings were never tracked down. But it is intrinsically probable that radical groups, for whom the official Reformation had stopped half-way, were meeting in the capital. Whether they then deliberately withdrew from the communion of the Established Church cannot be ascertained. A more visible and substantial organization of a similar nature was that identified by the Privy Council in the village of Bocking in Essex at the end of 1550. This group, of which about a dozen members were arrested and interrogated, seems to have been one of a network spreading over Kent and Essex, with meetings in Maidstone, Faversham and Ashford. The original purpose of these meetings seems to have been Bible study and discussion, rather like the Lollard conventicles with which they had much in common; but by the time the authorities acted, a distinctive doctrinal position had begun to emerge. Official protestantism was strongly predestinarian, which was a natural, if not inevitable, step from justification *sola fide* (by faith alone), but these people rejected that step, and were consequently known as the Free-willers. (**97, chs. 3 and 4**) The Freewillers had their own fund-raisers, and an acknowledged leader in the person of Henry Hart. They had also withdrawn themselves deliberately from the communion of the Established Church, and were thus authentic, if somewhat embryonic, separatists. After Edward's death they became, along with the orthodox protestants, the victims of Mary's policy of catholic restoration. In prison in London, Hart conducted a vigorous dispute with John Bradford, much to the amusement of the catholic authorities, and was not prepared to join him in communion unless a doctrinal agreement could be reached.

Although some Freewillers may have continued to meet at liberty during Mary's reign, the majority of conventicles which can be identified used the Edwardian prayer book, and were therefore neither radical nor sectarian in principle. 'The usage is to have all the English services without any diminishing, wholly as it was in the time of King Edward VI', wrote one government agent. An exception was the congregation visited by the pamphleteer Miles Huggarde in Islington, some time in 1555. If Huggarde's admittedly biased description is at all accurate, this was an organized group, led by a radical preacher whom he called 'Father Brown' (in *The Displaying of the Protestants*, 1556). It had a recognized membership, and would not admit strangers. Brown preached, rather like John Harrydance, quoting long passages of scripture from memory, and denounced 'my Lord Chancellor's religion' (catholicism) and 'Cranmer's, Latimer's and Ridley's religion' (protestantism) with fine impartiality. According to Huggarde, Brown attracted a large audience from all over London, a circumstance which aroused the author's scorn and indignation. Another radical group was apparently meeting in Colchester during these years, but it has left only circumstantial evidence of its existence. It has been claimed that many of Foxe's martyrs were radicals and would have been persecuted by a protestant government, but this is hard to substantiate. Some were individual eccentrics, and a few little better than hooligans, but there is little evidence of sectarian dissent in the pages of the *Acts and Monuments*.

In the 1580s, when small-scale protestant separatism was an established fact, some of those then involved looked back to the clandestine congregations of Mary's reign for their origin, but this was almost certainly wishful thinking, because the protestant dissent which existed in the early years of Elizabeth's reign was of quite a different nature. There were conventicles, one in the Minories outside Aldgate, and another at Plumbers Hall; but they were radical only in the sense of wishing to go further in the elimination of 'popery'. In other words, they were discontented puritans, whose objective was further reform, not separation. There were those who doubted the validity of the royal supremacy and would have preferred a more scriptural discipline, but they did not see themselves as a 'gathered' church. Later in the reign the Family of Love had members in London, but they were more like the 'known men' of the fifteenth century than the contemporary Hutterites and Mennonites of central Europe. (**97, chs. 10 and 12**) Radicalism in the true sense had only a fitful and uncertain existence in England during the formative years of the Reformation, and when it came it was more the result of disillusionment with the establishment than of any positive sense of a special revelation. Radicalism, or Anabaptism, was a bogy with which the ecclesiastical authorities regularly frightened themselves, particularly when they wanted to urge the secular government to tougher discipline, but when it is investigated, it usually turns out to be the ale-house pronouncements of a few unconnected individuals.

c) The strength of traditional piety

All the spontaneous moves towards Reformation in the English Church were the work of vocal but small minorities. Even in London, where Lollard cells were followed by protestant preachers and iconoclastic congregations, some parishes maintained their conservative traditions well into Elizabeth's reign. There were 106 parish churches in the city, and as Susan Brigden has demonstrated in her major study of Reformation London, their wide varieties of practice and tradition are hard to account for. (51) [**DOCUMENT IV, iii**] There was no obvious connection between prosperity and religious stance, but certain crafts — particularly weaving and printing — were heavily represented among the early reformers and the Merchant Adventurers were generally sympathetic. It was in the Adventurers' Antwerp house that William Tyndale found refuge when he was in trouble with the ecclesiastical authorities, and his financial backer, Humphrey Monmouth, was also a member. Nevertheless, it seems to

have been the predilections of individuals, and particularly of individual clergy, which initiated these distinctive attitudes. The
Church of St Martin in Ironmonger Lane was stripped of its rood and
images within a few days of Henry VIII's death through the zeal of
its reforming rector, John Handyman, and his churchwardens.
Handyman had anticipated official policy by over a year, and the
Council made him replace the images for the time being, but his
personal responsibility for this move seems to be clear. On the other
hand, within a month of Mary's accession in 1553, and long before the
official Church settlement had been changed, 'began the mass at St
Nicholas Cole Abbey, goodly sung in Latin', and within a few days
four or five other city churches had followed the same course 'not by
commandment but of the people's devotion'. By contrast, in another
parish an old priest who tried to take a similar initiative was set upon
and almost lynched. On Elizabeth's accession the forces in London
were probably about equal, but over the next twenty years steady
official pressure reduced the conservative presence to a hard core of
catholic recusancy. By 1580 the city had strongly puritan parishes and
conservative Anglican parishes, while recusant conventicles survived
with difficulty. Catholic attempts to maintain a secret printing press
in London were short-lived and unsuccessful.

In the realm as a whole the balance was very different. Although
there were towns, such as Colchester and Chelmsford, and villages,
such as Hadleigh in Suffolk, where protestant congregations were
strongly established by the end of Edward's reign, the general picture ·
is one of conservative preference and reluctant conformity. The rebuilding and embellishment of churches went on vigorously, right
down to the 1540s; St Michael-le-Belfry in York, Launceston
(Cornwall), Great Panton (Lincolnshire) and Barton-under-
Nedwood (Staffordshire) are examples of churches completely rebuilt
between 1500 and 1540. (22) The evidence of wills also suggests a
widespread enthusiasm for the traditional pieties. A Cambridgeshire
woman, dying in about 1530, left small sums of money to the high
altar, the bells and torches, and the repair fund of her parish church,
13s.4d. to 'Our Lady's light', and pieces of plate to two confraternities
in the parish. Such examples could be endlessly multiplied. During an
episcopate lasting from 1506 to 1522, Bishop Fitzjames of London
ordained 840 men, an average of sixty a year. Between 1540 and 1547
Bishop Bonner ordained a mere forty-six, and during Edward's reign
the numbers fell still further. Significantly, there was a marked
recovery under Mary. Nor are the reasons very far to seek. Ritual and

ceremony brought colour to drab lives, and comfort amid the constant uncertainties of mortality. To make confession and receive the viaticum was to die in peace. In a world with no scientific understanding of causality, supernatural forces were seen to be constantly active. Consecrated objects afforded protection, and the saints were credible intercessors with a God who was hardly accessible to the imagination of anyone who was not a mystic. The desire to humanize the divine can be seen most clearly in the cult of the Virgin Mary. Mary — the only female principal in the holy story — represented the mercy of God, and her shrines at Walsingham, Caversham and many other places were constantly resorted to. In theory, images, stained-glass windows and pictures of sacred subjects were aids to devotion; in fact, they were often icons — objects of veneration in themselves. Because of the peculiar devotion paid to the consecrated host, the mass was seen as an effective means of reconciling conflicting factions and individuals. In 1459 a riot in Fleet Street had been pacified by the appearance of clergy bearing a cross and pyx, and there are numerous references to quarrelling neighbours setting aside their disputes in order to make the kiss of peace and receive the sacrament.

Such visible and tangible signs of devotion were hard to replace in the language of the new faith. A man who lit a candle to the Virgin would feel assured that the prayer which that candle represented would be heard and transmitted to Christ in a way which only his mother could do. To put his petition into his own words and address it direct would seem presumptuous, and probably quite ineffective. After all, if you wanted to address a petition to the king, or to a great lord, you approached him through one of his servants or councillors. To intrude upon his presence unbidden would be to invite rejection — or worse. For the great majority of ordinary people, the Church was identified by what it did rather than by what it taught. By comparison, protestantism was verbal and intellectual; it required its devotees to know their Bible and to accept abstract principles like justification by faith alone. Such a doctrine might provide emancipation for an over-active conscience, but it might equally remove the landmarks of everyday piety. Similarly, in a culture which judged so much by appearances, a shrine glittering with gold and jewels was like a king in his coronation robes, impressive by virtue of sheer magnificence and unimaginable cost. If God was the king of kings, then everything associated with him must be splendid, and if he was not then his power as a protector and patron had to be doubted. The Church had always understood human need for the ritual and the tangible, and it could be argued that it had grown fat on that knowledge; but those who defended the wealth of the Church did so on the grounds that it needed the trappings of power to impose its moral authority. So many Englishmen clung to their traditional ceremonies, to their processions and holy water, and above all to the mass, long after the legislation of Elizabeth's first Parliament had finally made such things illegal. (17, ch. 9) [DOCUMENT I, viii] The queen had some sympathy with them, and retained the cross on her own chapel communion table. She also seems to have understood, in a way which some of her more zealously protestant councillors and bishops did not, that this kind of conservatism did not necessarily imply a devotion to the Pope — let alone to Habsburg political interests. After 1570, when the mass became a symbol of a potentially treasonable allegiance, such indulgence disappeared, but by that time the Anglican Church was beginning to find its own ways of coping with liturgical nostalgia.

d) The literate tradition: puritanism

The Lollards had been great readers, not only of English scripture, but also of tracts such as *Jack up Land* and *The Lantern of Light*, highly critical of many orthodox practices. One of the commonest charges brought against those suspected of heresy in the pre-Reformation period had been the possession of these books. Richard Hun, according to Foxe the protomartyr of the English Reformation, had been accused for that reason in 1514. Hun was a man of some education, but the Lollard tradition in general was not a learned one after its very early days, and the frequent references to books do not mean that the majority of these dissenters were literate. The normal practice was for one person to read aloud to the group, and the retentive memories of the hearers often enabled them to repeat long passages verbatim, giving a false impression of literacy to the investigating authorities. (37) Although printing was introduced to England by William Caxton in 1476, the Lollards had no access to the press, and the majority of early printers were Flemings or Frenchmen — such as Richard Pynson and Wynkyn de Worde — who had no interest in English religious controversies, and were very anxious to keep out of trouble. It was not the Lollards but the Lutherans who first used the press for polemical purposes, a skill which was highly developed in Germany before it made any impact on England. Also, unlike Lollardy, the new German and Swiss ideas were first influential in the universities, and their early promoters, men like John Frith and Robert Barnes, were academic preachers. The gap between these two traditions was bridged to some extent in the 1530s by the printing of some eleven or twelve Wycliffite works in London and Antwerp, but thereafter the older influence was submerged by a steadily increasing tide of protestant polemical and devotional books. When it first appeared in 1539, the Great Bible was used in much the same way as the old Lollard scriptures, but a new incentive to literacy had been created, and the educational picture had begun to change. There is no means of judging what proportion of the population could read in 1540. Sir Thomas More argued against an English Bible on the grounds that more than 70 per cent were illiterate, and he may have been understating the case. On the other hand, thanks to humanist influence at court, education for the gentry and aristocracy had become a *sine qua non* for royal service, and led to higher expectations at all levels of society.

John Foxe attributed the success of the Reformation, in contrast with the relative failure of Wycliffe, to the fact that 'God had opened the press to preach', and the strenuous censorship attempted by conservative authorities, both under Henry VIII and Mary, suggests that they shared the same view. Bishop Nix of Norwich is alleged to have said, with reference to Tyndale's New Testament, '. . . it will undo us all'. Thanks partly to the patronage of Thomas Cromwell, and partly to political circumstances, the reformers had seized the publishing initiative before Henry VIII's death, although explicitly protestant works still had to be printed abroad. Hard-hitting polemic, such as John Bale's *The Image of Both Churches*, Henry Brinkelow's *The Complaint of Roderyke Mors*, and William Turner's *Hunting and Finding Out of the Romish Fox*, found a ready market; and one of the main reasons why cities such as London, Bristol and Newcastle-upon-Tyne were showing strong signs of protestant influence by 1547 was the high literacy rate demanded by a commercial centre. Significantly, the accession of Edward VI was followed almost immediately by an explosion of literary activity in the capital. Within a year the number of presses had gone up from twenty-five to thirty-nine, and the number of titles printed from about 100 to 225 per annum. (**20, ch. 6**) The great bulk of this increase was accounted for by protestant works at various levels, from a translation of Calvin's *A Faithful and Most Godly Treatise* down to scurrilous pieces like *The Upcheringe of the Mass*. For the first time England had an equivalent of the German *flügschriften* (fly-sheets) of the 1520s, and although the earlier practice of reading aloud undoubtedly continued, it is equally clear that there was a sizeable market of the semi-educated, particularly in and around London. The euphoria of 1547/8 did not last, and by 1552 publishing activity had returned to something like its late-Henrician level, but it was a trade controlled almost entirely by protestants, and beginning to show marked signs of extremism.

Mary's conservative revolution of 1553 reduced the number of printers by almost half, and the number of titles by about the same. Catholic propaganda and polemic appeared for the first time, but did not match either the quantity or the quality of the protestant output under Edward. Instead, the protestants took the initiative abroad with them and, after a hesitant start, their attacks upon the queen became increasingly strident and radical. Exile and persecution were traumatic experiences for men who had become accustomed to a protestant establishment, and many of them did not know quite how to react. They took the Prayer Book abroad with them, and at Zurich, Strasbourg and Frankfurt established congregations with the 'face' of an English church, but they could not export the royal supremacy, and resorted instead to an uneasy form of independency. Elizabeth's accession was their salvation. They were able to fit back into a protestant establishment, and the Anglican future belonged to them. But some of their colleagues, who tackled their dilemma more positively and energetically, were less fortunate. Even among Edward's bishops there had been men, like John Hooper, for whom the model of reformation was in Switzerland rather than in England. During the exile several such men took refuge in Geneva and in Aarau, establishing there churches which followed the disciplinary and liturgical principles of John Calvin. It was in Geneva that Christopher Goodman published *How Superior Powers Ought to be Obeyed*, a work which not only declared it to be a religious duty for the Godly to arise and overthrow Mary, but also suggested a church order to which the monarchy was virtually an irrelevance. Had protestantism been restored to England by any means other than Elizabeth's accession, the Genevan model might very well have been followed. Such men as Whittingham and Gilby did not object to the royal supremacy, provided that the Supreme Governor measured up to their standards of godliness, and they spent the next thirty years in the second rank of the English Church, trying to insist on that condition. These were the men usually known as puritans, for whom the Bible was all important, and who carried the abstract and intellectual principles of protestantism further than their less strenuous colleagues. They brought back with them a new English Bible, printed in Geneva, and an enthusiasm for protracted scriptural sermons. It was among the puritans that the literate tradition of protestantism found its fullest expression, in a style of worship devoid of music, ritual or colour. There was no such thing as an illiterate puritan, and the appeal of the movement was consequently restricted, but they formed the theological front line against the Counter-Reformation, and became strong at court and in the universities. Until the 1570s, they could be described as a minority within a minority, but unlike the true radicals (who tended to be anti-intellectual) they made themselves extremely influential by working within the system. Although they considered natural science to be a presumptuous human meddling with the divine order, their extreme contempt for magical or 'superstitious' explanations created a climate of opinion in which a secular rationalism could later flourish.

6.　　Continental Influences

a) Germany

Luther's influence in England lay rather in the example which he had set than in any specific doctrine which he taught. Some of his writings, probably the *Reply to Prierias* and *Resolutiones Disputationum*, were being read and discussed in Cambridge as early as 1518, two years before his condemnation. The members of this university group were interested in him because of the stand which he had taken against the abuse of indulgences and papal authority, rather than because of his views on justification, which were not explicit at that point. They saw him at first as an ally of Erasmus and the other humanist critics of the Church, with whom they were already strongly in sympathy. However, within a few years the logical connection between the theology of good works and many of the abuses of which they complained had moved some of them, notably Thomas Bilney, Robert Barnes and Hugh Latimer, in the direction of justification by faith alone. They were not 'Lutherans' in the later sense, and Barnes in particular continued to believe in transubstantiation, but they were heretics in the eyes of the Church. Barnes was arrested soon after Christmas 1525 for a sermon abusing Wolsey, and for teaching some radical ideas on the social responsibility of Christians which certainly owed nothing to Luther. He recanted, but soon after was caught distributing copies of Tyndale's New Testament. Condemned as a relapsed heretic, he contrived to escape to Antwerp, from whence, in 1529, he made his way to Wittenburg. Barnes's position was not unique, but it was exceptional. The main reaction to the new German teaching among educated Englishmen was hostile, exemplified by the king's *Assertio Septem Sacramentorum*, which was published in several editions after 1521, and in the sermons of John Fisher. Erasmus's already strong influence carried the majority with him in his dispute with Luther over free will in 1525.

The first English translation of a work by Luther seems to have been William Roy's rendering of his commentary upon St Paul's Epistle to the Corinthians (1529), and there was nothing like the popular demand which kept the German presses so busy throughout the 1520s. William Tyndale's New Testament, which did attract such demand, may have owed something to Luther's example, but nothing to his own version. In 1528, when a heretical cell was uncovered in Oxford, its reading matter consisted not only of Luther and Melanchthon, but also Oecolampadius, Zwingli, Bugenhagen, Bucer, Urbanus Rhegius and several others. Even those Englishmen who visited Wittenburg during these years seem to have treated Luther simply as one source of ideas among many. One temporary exception to this generalization was Robert Barnes. While still in Wittenburg in 1531, he published a *Supplication to King Henry the eight* which has been described as a mere translation and paraphrase of his master. However, even Barnes's Lutheran orthodoxy did not last, and when he published a second edition of his *Supplication* in 1534, it differed in a number of respects from the line laid down by the Confession of Augsburg. Henry's own hostility to Luther was never overcome, even after he had broken with Rome and was looking favourably upon other reformers; and the German's outspoken contempt for 'Junker Harry' made many Englishmen who might otherwise have been sympathetic look elsewhere for inspiration. Another obstacle to his influence was his complex and conservative interpretation of the eucharistic presence. On this issue Luther was at odds with virtually every other reformer, and the English preferred a simpler doctrine of the Real Presence. It was Swiss rather than German ideas which were expressed in the Prayer Book of 1552 and the Forty-two Articles. [**DOCUMENTS III, v; V, ii; V, iii**] For that reason, Lutheran towns, such as Wesel, refused asylum to the Marian exiles, and thereby lost their last chance (as it turned out) of influencing the eventual Elizabethan settlement. In the later years of the sixteenth century, a small handful of English clergy discreetly persisted in their preference for some of Luther's teaching, but they had no significant influence. Objections to the Confession of Augsburg also obstructed Elizabeth's hopes for improved relations with the German princes in the 1560s.

Somewhat paradoxically, in view of this catalogue of failures, Thomas Cranmer owed a lot to the German reformers — not to Luther specifically, but rather to Bugenhagen and Oecolampadius. His diplomatic mission to Germany in 1532 in search of an elusive Charles V was a turning-point in his career. Already convinced of the unlawfulness of papal authority (and therefore high in the king's favour), and of the need for vernacular scriptures, Cranmer found the worship of the Lutheran congregations a revelation. Here was a church with an impressive vernacular liturgy; a church which had already got rid of its religious houses and redistributed the property to charity and education; a church with married clergy. This last was a point of some personal importance to Cranmer. As a young fellow of Jesus College, Cambridge, he had jeopardized his career by marrying and thus having to resign his fellowship. His wife had died within a year, and he had subsequently been ordained. However, like Thomas More, he recognized that he did not have the gift of prolonged chastity. To More, that had been a reason for not entering the priesthood; but to Cranmer it was an argument for married clergy. While in Germany he took the extraordinary step of a secret marriage to Margaret, the niece of the Lutheran divine Andreas Osiander, who probably performed the ceremony. A few months later, he returned from his mission to find himself nominated to the archbishopric of Canterbury! It is hardly surprising that he accepted the preferment with reluctance. Margaret was a hostage to fortune, and it is reasonably certain that Henry VIII learned of her existence long before his death, but he never allowed her to be used against the Archbishop. This was partly because he recognized that Cranmer was not, in any substantial sense, a Lutheran. It is not known when Cranmer became converted to justification by faith alone, because he kept his views to himself until 1547, and he never accepted Luther's doctrine of the eucharist. Until 1547 he was as loyal to the mass as Henry himself, which was one of the main reasons for the king's continued confidence in him; and thereafter he was converted to the Swiss view. (**4, Vol. VIII, p. 62**) When he came to compose his own English liturgy in 1548/9, it was mainly a translation of the traditional Sarum rite. The Lutheran liturgies had provided the example, but only to a very small extent the model. Some of the more zealous Swiss reformers continued to accuse him of holding German views, but that was true only to the extent that Luther's doctrine of justification, for example, had become the common property of the protestant world. In the event, the political circumstances of the English Reformation created a church order which resembled those of Germany and Scandinavia rather than of Zurich or Geneva, but its doctrine owed little to the Confession of Augsburg. In most respects, Thomas Cranmer was his own man, and it was his influence rather than that of Luther which was reflected in the worship of the Anglican Church.

b) Switzerland

Ulrich Zwingli, the original reformer of Zurich, had died at the Battle of Kappel in 1533, and there is little sign of his direct influence in England. In many respects his doctrine resembled that of Luther, although he denied being a follower of the Wittenberg reformer, and advocated a much closer relationship with the secular authorities. He had also received a humanist rather than a scholastic education, and took a more austere view of worship. The main point of disagreement between them, however, was over the eucharistic presence. [DOCUMENT V, ii] It was that issue which frustrated the attempt at Marburg in 1529 to create a single protestant front to present to the catholic Church in the show-down which was clearly coming. When Heinrich Bullinger succeeded Zwingli in 1533, he therefore took over an independent church, not in communion with those of Saxony or Hesse, and very closely identified with the magistrates of the canton of Zurich. On the other hand, he also inherited a sphere of influence which extended into South Germany and the Rhineland, and which had produced the independent Tetrapolitan Confession in 1530. (The four cities were Strasbourg, Constance, Memmingen and Lindau.) Bullinger was an amiable and hospitable man, and an indefatigable correspondent. Throughout the remainder of his life, which lasted until 1572, he entertained a stream of visitors from all over Europe, and built up contacts as far apart as Poland and Scotland. His links with England seem to have begun in 1536, when his friend Martin Bucer of Strasbourg commended a group of young Englishmen to his attention. London had long-standing trade links with the Rhineland, via Antwerp, and it seems to have been business rather than the search for theological enlightenment which had brought John Butler, Nicholas Partridge and William Woodroffe to Strasbourg. Nevertheless, they were clearly members of the reforming 'connection' in the city, and went home equally impressed by Bullinger's teaching and his hospitality. Over the next few years the connection was developed. Bartholomew Traheron, John Burcher and a number of others trod the same path, while Rudolph Gualther, Bullinger's foster-son, made the journey in the opposite direction.

The reasons why the English found Bullinger's teaching congenial can only be guessed, but probably they had something to do with his low-key views on the eucharistic presence. In 1499 two Lollard priests had declared that only pure bread was present in a consecrated host, and in 1528 another had stated that '. . . the body of Christ [is] in the word and not in the bread'. This was exactly the doctrine which Bullinger had taken over from Zwingli. Richard Hilles, the young merchant tailor who withdrew to Strasbourg in 1541, after the Act of Six Articles, and was a busy contact man between London and Switzerland for the remainder of the decade, had first got into trouble with the ecclesiastical authorities for writing a commentary on the Epistle of James. The issue was good works, and his inspiration may have been German, but the Epistle of James was also a favourite Lollard text. Hilles was a layman, and a follower rather than a leader, but one of those who benefited from the connections which he had established was John Hooper. The origin of Hooper's protestantism is not known, but by 1545 his outspokenness had brought him into danger, and he retreated first to Basle and then to Zurich. When he returned to England in 1549, he had adopted the Zwinglian position on a range of issues, but a recent scholar discussing his theology has called him a Lollard. (86) In some respects the distinction was a fine one. When Hooper found himself at odds with the protestant establishment in England over the issue of vestments, which he regarded as 'Aaronical' and 'popish rags', Bullinger urged a commonsense moderation upon him for the good of the Church. The latter warmly welcomed a group of refugees from the Marian persecution, and allowed them to continue using their own Prayer Book (a document of which he did not entirely approve) in Zurich, as something appertaining to their own tradition. In 1563, after Elizabeth's accession, he was again appealed to on the issue of vestments, and advised that this was a matter which could safely be left to the discretion of the Godly Magistrate. Bullinger's enthusiasm for the Godly Prince, and his willingness to accept the royal supremacy as being compatible with a true church in England, undoubtedly made the Elizabethan settlement easier to establish. His credentials with the puritans were impeccable, and his influence was used in the direction of peace and moderation.

Bullinger's irenicism was demonstrated most convincingly in a move which had nothing directly to do with England. In 1549 he negotiated a concordat with the neighbouring church of Geneva known as the *Consensus Tigurinus*. John Calvin had come to his own conclusions on most doctrinal issues, and Bullinger made the larger number of concessions in reaching agreement, but the result did no violence to the consciences of either side, and enabled the Swiss to present a united front to both the catholics and the Lutherans. This united church is usually known by Calvin's name, because it was

Calvin's *Institutes of the Christian Religion* which provided its most complete and systematic exposition of doctrine and discipline, but as long as he lived Bullinger's influence was at least the equal of Calvin's. In his relations with the Church in England, moreover, Calvin backed the wrong horse. He disliked the 1552 Prayer Book, and despised the lack of congregational discipline in the English establishment. The English congregations which came under his influence during the Marian exile rejected the Prayer Book in favour of the Genevan order, and lost a head-to-head conflict in Frankfurt with those who wanted to preserve a more distinctive English identity. From the printing presses of Geneva came not only Goodman's *How Superior Powers*, but also John Knox's *First Blast of the Trumpet against the Monstrous Regiment of Women*. Understandably, Knox was anathema to Elizabeth, and Calvin's lack of enthusiasm for the Godly Prince did nothing to commend his system to her attention. Those who returned to England inspired by the example of 'the most Godly church' were doomed to disappointment. The official doctrine of the Anglican Church, set out in the Thirty-nine Articles of 1566, has been described as Calvinist, but it would be more accurate to describe it as broadly reformed and somewhat eclectic. Those who adhered strictly to the views of Calvin were the Presbyterians, who made a considerable impact in the 1570s and 1580s, and again in the 1640s, but who failed to gain control as long as the royal supremacy was in working order. John Calvin was probably the most respected and influential theologian throughout the protestant world in the later sixteenth century (**DOCUMENT V, iv**), but his following in England was restricted to a minority among the clergy and the educated gentry. Neither public policy nor popular tradition was moulded in accordance with his wishes.

c) The Low Countries

By the early sixteenth century, the Netherlands had long been a seed-bed of religious dissent. The *Devotio Moderna* had established its influence strongly in the fifteenth century, and the Brethren of the Common Life had a number of schools and communities at Deventer and elsewhere. It was from this background that Erasmus of Rotterdam emerged to be the most influential scholar and educationalist in northern Europe between 1500 and 1530. The south-east of England was in constant contact with the trading centres of Flanders and Brabant, and there was a broad diffusion of reforming ideas from this source, particularly among merchant and artisan groups. There was also a strong radical tradition, which gained momentum from the developments in Germany, and particularly the emergence of leaders such as Andreas Carlstadt and Thomas Müntzer between 1520 and 1525. Alarmed by the great Peasants' Revolt of the latter year, the authorities everywhere clamped down on radicalism, and no one more rigorously than Charles V in the Netherlands. This had the effect of forcing some of the radicals back into Germany where, under the leadership of Jan of Leyden, they played a conspicuous part in the Anabaptist 'kingdom' of Munster in 1534. Others took refuge in England where, until the advent of Thomas More as Lord Chancellor in 1530, persecution had been low-key and sporadic. More's tenure was brief, and although persecution continued thereafter, it was on a much smaller scale than in the Low Countries. Consequently hundreds, perhaps thousands, of Dutch and Flemish artisans and craftsmen lived and worked in London, Norwich, and other towns within easy reach of their original homes. Considering their numbers, and the radical nature of some of their ideas, they attracted remarkably little attention. Some of them, it was alleged, believed that Christian men should hold all goods in common, others that Christ took no flesh of his mother, others that the human soul is mortal. A few were denounced, and feature in the ecclesiastical records, and a handful, such as Jan Mattijs, George Van Parris, and the fourteen victims of the purge of 1535, were burned. An unknown number may have suffered, like Anneke Jans, if they ventured to return to the Netherlands. The fact that they were largely left in peace suggests that they got on well enough with their English neighbours, which was no mean feat within a decade of the Evil May Day, but they had little impact on the religious life of the communities in which they lived. An Englishman identified only as 'Henry' turned up at Bergholt in 1536 professing Anabaptist views which seem to have been of Continental rather than Lollard origin, but such cases are extremely rare. An elusive Anabaptist 'bishop', a Fleming called Bastiane, also flits through the records, but he seems to have been no more than a casual visitor and was never apprehended.

Much more significant for the English Reformation was the role of Netherlands towns, such as Emden and Middleburg, but above all Antwerp, in the publication of English-language books. (**20, ch. 6**) The houses of Hoochstraten, Crom and Ruremond produced dozens of protestant works in English between 1530 and 1550; and although some were also produced in Bonn, Strasbourg and Zurich, Antwerp was by far the largest centre. The commercial links with London were strong, and smuggling was easy, as can be seen from the evidence of the occasional trader who was caught, like Robert Necton. The ecclesiastical authorities in Brabant, so zealous against their own heretics, were for a long time remarkably indifferent to this trade, perhaps because the language guaranteed that the books would not be read at home. The jurisdictional privileges of Antwerp may also have played a part in the immunity. After 1547 the situation changed and several Low Countries printers who had specialized in the English market, such as Stephen Mierdman and Giles Van der Erve, actually moved their businesses to London. By 1550 there was a Dutch 'Strangers' Church' at the Austin Friars, with a chartered immunity from the jurisdiction of the Bishop of London. The members of this church were not radicals, but protestants broadly in the Swiss tradition, and its pastor was the exiled Pole, John Lasco. (61) These Strangers' churches (another was granted to the French community) were not well received by Bishop Nicholas Ridley or by Archbishop Cranmer. Although their doctrine was broadly the same as that of the English Church, many of their practices were different and they did not use the Prayer Book, although translations were provided for their use. Ridley feared that they would provide models for licensed nonconformity which their English neighbours would wish to imitate. In fact, he need not have worried, because they seem to have had very little influence, except perhaps upon those English who became fugitives in their turn a few years later.

Other Strangers' churches existed outside London, notably in Norwich, but the only one to enjoy a privileged status was the group of Walloon weavers who were settled in the dissolved abbey at Glastonbury by Protector Somerset. The pastor of this congregation was the Frenchman, Valerand Poullain. None of these churches long survived Mary's accession. By 16 August 1553 the foreign pastors had been forbidden to preach, and the services at Austin Friars and Threadneedle Street came to an end. Early in September the Glastonbury community was expelled by the Privy Council, and on 17 September Lasco and 175 of the Dutch congregation took ship for Denmark. Shortly after, Lasco himself moved on to Emden in Friesland, where he ministered until his return to Poland in 1556. Although their church had been closed and they faced an uncertain future in London, many of the Dutch community remained, in defiance of a royal proclamation ordering all non-denizens to depart.

They were able to do this largely because of the connivance, even protection, of the city authorities. With the religious situation in the Netherlands continuing to deteriorate after Philip of Spain took over from his father Charles in August 1555, they had little incentive to abandon what was still in effect a refuge. The protestant printers Van der Erve and Mierdman could not expect similar indulgence; they were marked men, and both made haste to depart to the security of Emden. With the accession of Elizabeth, the Dutch (and other Strangers' churches) swiftly reappeared. As under Edward, the Privy Council was actively supportive, not only because it wished to advertise England's return to the reformed faith, but also for sound economic reasons. The Glastonbury congregation was not resurrected, but Austin Friars reopened its doors in June 1560, and in the following year a new church was established on William Cecil's initiative at Sandwich in Kent. A few years later, Flemish silk-weavers were encouraged to settle in Norwich, and the longstanding connection of that city with the Netherlands was explicitly recognized. Ironically, when the government had been hostile to the Dutch, the Londoners had protected them, but when the government encouraged them to settle in significant numbers, the artisans of the city were not pleased and considerable friction ensued.

Because of their proximity, the development of persecution in their homeland, and the similarity of their faith to English protestantism, the Netherlanders became after 1540 the most numerous, and also the most economically constructive, of the refugee communities, but they do not seem to have had much more influence on the English Reformation than their Anabaptist predecessors of the previous generation. Almost as soon as the Dutch Church was re-established in 1560, it became convulsed with a dispute over renewed infiltration by Anabaptists, and some members of the Family of Love also settled in England under the broad umbrella of the Netherlandish community. (**97, p. 180**) Both were strongly disapproved of by the Elizabethan Church, but remained exotic elements which evoked little or no response from a population still attempting to come to terms with the results of two decades of their own upheavals. The Dutch community had many influential preachers and writers in the course of its existence in London, but produced no reforming leader of the first rank, and the Netherlands Church as a whole did not produce a Bullinger, let alone a Calvin — or a Cranmer.

d) Others

During the brief reign of Edward VI, England became a refuge for persecuted protestants from all over Europe. In addition to the Dutch church at Austin Friars, the French community was given the use of the chapel of St Anthony in Threadneedle Street, with similar privileges, and there were smaller groups of Germans, Italians and even Spaniards. In 1550 five parishes in London counted 'strangers' as 10 per cent of the adult male population, and two had more than 20 per cent. Norwich, Southampton, Bristol and other large commercial centres also had their alien communities, although not all these were of religious refugees. Once it had become clear that Elizabeth was restoring the Edwardian situation, the fugitives appeared again, the Huguenots becoming particularly numerous as France drifted into civil war. However, in one respect the experience of Edward's reign was not repeated. In 1548, following his victory over the Schmalkaldic League at the Battle of Muhlberg, Charles V endeavoured to impose a religious settlement upon the protestants of Germany and the Rhineland. This so-called Interim was largely ineffective, but it temporarily dislodged a number of leading reformers from their normal bases. Cranmer, partly repaying his own debts, and partly looking for assistance in the uphill task of evangelizing England, invited several of them to cross the Channel. Some of the most important, such as Philip Melanchthon, declined; others accepted, of whom the most significant were the Italian Peter Martyr Vermigli and Martin Bucer of Strasbourg. Martyr was given a chair at Oxford, and Bucer at Cambridge, and both became extremely influential teachers. Bucer had the more congenial context, thanks to reforming traditions going back to the White Horse group in the 1520s, and his lectures were still spoken of with enthusiasm twenty years later, but his time was short. He was an elderly man, and the fenland climate killed him in 1551. [**DOCUMENT V, iii**] Martyr, facing much stronger conservative hostility, nevertheless succeeded in building up a useful reforming group, particularly in Magdalen and Brasenose Colleges. He was driven out by his enemies immediately after Mary's accession and, after a brief stay in London, retreated to the Continent before the end of 1553. Thanks to the Elizabethan settlement, which brought their pupils to positions of influence in both universities, the brief stay of these two notable scholars had an important impact on the English Church.

For the same reason, 'strangers' who occupied similar positions

during Mary's reign left very little memory behind them. When
Philip II came to England in July 1554, he brought his own chaplains
and confessors with him. Some of these, such as Alonso á Castro and
Bartolomé Carranza, remained at court, where they probably
exercised considerable influence over ecclesiastical policy. Carranza
remained to work with Cardinal Pole after Philip's departure in 1555,
and may have been instrumental in maintaining the policy of persecution. Two, however, went to Oxford, Pedro de Soto and Juan de Villa
Garcia. There they occupied chairs until they were driven out by the
Elizabethan settlement. Generally speaking, neither Mary nor Pole
was sympathetic to the theology and spirituality of the Counter-
Reformation, but de Soto and Villa Garcia were steeped in that
tradition, and their teaching conveyed it to their pupils. In spite of (or
perhaps because of) the conservative atmosphere of Oxford, these
Spaniards were no more welcome than Peter Martyr had been, and no
assessment of their influence has ever been made. A number of
Oxford catholics withdrew to the Continent in the early years of
Elizabeth's reign, and their decisions may well have resulted from
exposure to such teaching. The recusant tradition owed a lot to Pole's
effective visitation of the universities, and the appointment of these
two learned Spanish friars has to be seen in that context.

As we have seen, other Continental reformers, notably Valerand
Poullain and John Lasco, worked in England during Edward's reign,
and helped to keep the English Church in touch with other reforming
movements. A number of Swiss students, such as John and Conrad
ab Ulmis, also spent some time in the English universities, and
conducted a lively and informative correspondence with their fellow
countrymen. (8) But the most important of the scholarly visitors was
undoubtedly Martin Bucer, and this was not so much on account of
his work in Cambridge as because of his relationship with Cranmer
and his stature among the Continental reformers before he came to
England. Bucer's approach was irenic and conciliatory. In his early
days in Strasbourg he had even attempted to tolerate the Anabaptists,
until convinced of the futility of such a gesture by their unmitigated
stridency and disruptiveness. He had endeavoured unsuccessfully to
mediate between Luther and Zwingli, and had played a leading role
in the Colloquy of Ratisbon in 1541, which had so nearly brought the
Lutheran schism to an end. In spite of his personal friendship with
Bullinger, the two men did not entirely see eye to eye, particularly
over eucharistic theology, and some of the more rigid Zwinglians
denounced him (quite unjustifiably) as a Lutheran. His strong belief

in a real, spiritual, presence in the elements, which caused such offence to the likes of Francis Dryander and John Hooper, commended him to Cranmer, and the Anglican position which eventually emerged was closer to his position than the Zurichers altogether liked. Bucer was also, along with Melanchthon, one of the main advocates of the concept of *adiaphora*, or 'things indifferent'. He believed that doctrine and practice could be broadly divided into two categories: those things which were necessary to be believed or done by the Elect as a testimony to their salvation, and those things which could be ordered in various ways according to local custom or the will of the magistrate. Logically, no constraints could be placed upon the Elect, since their salvation was predestined, but no reformers accepted that logic, which contained all sorts of sinister possibilities. So for all practical purposes certain beliefs — in the incarnation of Christ, the resurrection, and justification by faith alone — were necessary for salvation; and any hint of idolatry was a sure sign of reprobation. On the other hand, the nature of the liturgy, the dress of the clergy, and whether discipline was episcopal, synodal or congregational, could be safely and properly left to the Godly Magistrate to whom, like Bullinger, Bucer was very favourably inclined. Cranmer was not only temperamentally inclined in the same direction, he also welcomed a formula which enabled him to reconcile the royal supremacy with the demands of a godly reformation. In other words, Bucer was the ideal ally for the archbishop in the English situation, and the *Censurae* which he offered on the 1549 Prayer Book was the greatest single influence moving Cranmer further in the reformed direction — a movement publicly manifested in the 1550 Ordinal and the 1552 Prayer Book. The Anglican Church did not follow any single Continental model, but the two men who exercised the greatest influence, partly through Cranmer and partly direct to other Englishmen, were Heinrich Bullinger and Martin Bucer.

7.   The Legacy of Revolution

The dramatic events which took place between 1530 and 1570 permanently transformed the English Church and its relationship with secular society. Until the end of the sixteenth century, successive Popes campaigned vigorously for the recovery of the country; at first through Elizabeth's conversion, and later through her overthrow. Between 1568 and 1587 their preferred alternative was Mary, Queen of Scots; thereafter, it was the Infanta Isabella, daughter of Philip II of Spain. This campaign was conducted by an indiscriminate mixture of spiritual and political means, and it had two main consequences. The first was to confirm and intensify hatred of Rome, already apparent before the final triumph of protestantism; and the second was to identify English catholicism with treason against the state. The English catholics, throughout the later sixteenth and seventeenth centuries, were overwhelmingly loyal to the Crown, and deeply embarrassed by the manœuvres of their spiritual leaders on the Continent. A small minority entered wholeheartedly into the schemes of William Allen, Robert Parsons and their successors, thereby ensuring that the suspicions and hostility of the protestant government and ruling class were maintained. The spectre of reconversion from the top was raised briefly by the indiscreet behaviour of Charles I in the 1630s, and by the even more irresponsible conduct of James II between 1685 and 1688. In the first case the emotions which were stirred up played a major part in starting the civil war; in 1689 they provoked a bloodless coup, followed by constitutional changes which still exclude Catholics from the throne to the present day. Paradoxically, although none of the monarchs from Elizabeth to James II was a protestant crusader in the mould of Gaspar de Coligny or Gustavus Adolphus, it was its protestantism which identified England in the context of international relations as long as religion continued to be a factor at all. In the eighteenth century the priorities of the enlightenment and Britain's vastly increased commercial wealth gave it a new role, but the old hostilities lingered on into the industrial revolution, fuelled by the historical myth of the Elect.

During the peak years of the Reformation, the English protestants had set out to justify both their own activity and the royal supremacy by arguing that the realm of England had always enjoyed a special relationship with God. Some suggested that this went back to the Celtic church, some to King Lucius in the second century AD, and some to Joseph of Arimathea. The English were not alone in claiming a special providence, nor did it necessarily have anything to do with protestantism. The French had claimed it in the fifteenth century, the Spaniards claimed it in the sixteenth. However, in the case of England the point was slightly different. In the first place, it was necessary to argue that the evangelization of Britain went back before the mission of St Augustine of Canterbury in the sixth century, and was not the result of papal initiative. Secondly, the antiquity of the royal supremacy, assumed in the enacting statutes, needed to be historically demonstrated. King John became a key figure. Before John, so the argument ran, kings of England had run the Church, more or less without interference from Rome, although the contretemps between Henry II and Becket was a warning of the potentialities of clerical treason. John, however, had fallen victim to a conspiracy between the Pope, the French and his own rebellious subjects, and had been compelled to submit to papal authority. Since then the Pope's usurped supremacy had been maintained until Henry VIII had the courage and vision to return to the ways of his ancestors. As history this was palpable nonsense, confusing papal suzerainty with spiritual authority, but as myth it satisfied a pressing need. It also pointed towards a second argument, related but distinct. If the catholic Church had fallen into idolatry and become a false church at some point in the eleventh or twelfth century, where was the true church? The answer must lie among those whom the false church had persecuted — Godly Remnants identified with medieval heretics such as the Waldensians and Fraticelli. But there had to be a special role for England in this thesis also, which is how John Wycliffe became 'the morning star of the Reformation' — a role for which his teaching certainly gave him the right credentials. At the same time, the Statutes of Provisors and Praemunire became part of a worthy, if unsuccessful, attempt to shake off papal tyranny.

Unfortunately, as convinced protestants, neither John Bale nor John Foxe, who were the two principal architects of this historical myth, could claim that God worked in such a selective manner. John

Wycliffe may have been a divinely inspired agent of reform, but so were Martin Luther, Ulrich Zwingli and others who had no connection with either Wycliffe or England. England could not simply become the new Israel, the Elect Nation, however much some people may have longed for such a compelling vision. (83) As long as orthodox protestant eschatology prevailed, it was impossible to argue that a whole church, or nation, could have that status. The English Church was a true church, but only one among many with which it was in communion, and the most that could be claimed was that God had a special role in mind for the English as his purposes unfolded. Eventually myth was stronger than either history or theology, and one of the chief legacies of the Reformation to the imperial age of Great Britain was the sense of special providence. God, '. . . beneath whose awful hand we hold/dominion over palm and pine', was the creator and protector of an empire somewhat more extensive than that envisaged in the momentous statute of Henry VIII.

The English Church in 1530 was still adjusted, as it had been for some 800 years, to a feudal society with a strong sense of religious priority. In theory withdrawal from the world into a cloister was not merely acceptable, but an ideal form of Christian life; one, moreover, which had great value to the rest of humankind. By 1570 the monasteries had gone, and their lands had come to rest, very largely, in the hands of the lay aristocracy and the urban corporations. Bishops were no longer feudal magnates, and a visual, sacramental spirituality had been replaced by an educated and literate one. In other words, the English Church was adjusted to a gentry commonwealth under the Crown, and to a new aristocracy of law and commerce. That adjustment enabled the Church to remain a powerful establishment and a major force in national life down to the end of the nineteenth century. Protestantism was a faith which operated within the world, by seeking to influence its operations rather than by rejecting them, an adjustment which the catholic Church was also forced to make later, and with more difficulty. It could be argued that the Anglican Church under the royal supremacy was the ideal church for a society whose real priorities were elsewhere. At Edward VI's coronation in February 1547, Archbishop Thomas Cranmer declared that the role of the Church was to offer spiritual and moral guidance to the ruler, and to admonish him in God's name if he failed to achieve a satisfactory standard. But the Church had no commission to depose the king, or otherwise to limit the authority which God had given him. (12, pp. 469–70) That disclaimer remained valid; although the king gradually became the king-in-parliament, the relationship between the Church and the ruler did not change. Protestantism became a political rather than an ecclesiastical characteristic.

So the English Church emerged from the Reformation still for the most part catholic in its form, protestant in its doctrine and worship, and the servant rather than the master of secular society. There were those who were deeply unhappy with this transformation: not only the remaining catholics, but also those who took the sole authority of scripture with full seriousness. What happened, in the English situation, if the prince ceased to be Godly — or to make a passable pretence of being so? There was, indeed, no logical connection between protestantism and the royal supremacy, and it took a civil war and a constitutional revolution to make that connection *de iure* and effective. In many ways, politically and intellectually as well as spiritually, the Reformation left a great deal of uncompleted business. But its importance for the history of England, and Great Britain, extends far beyond the realms of ecclesiastical history.

Illustrative Documents

SECTION I: The Royal Supremacy

DOCUMENT I, i   The Act of Supremacy (extract)

The first statute inhibiting papal jurisdiction in England was the Act in Restraint of Appeals (1533). The positive claim to the royal supremacy was not made until the following year.

An Act concerning the King's Highness to be Supreme Head of the Church of England and to have authority to reform and redress all errors, heresies and abuses in the same (1534: 26 Henry VIII, c.I).

Albeit the King's Majesty justly and rightfully is and oweth to be the supreme head of the Church of England, and so is recognised by the clergy of this realm in their Convocations;[1] yet nevertheless for corroboration and confirmation thereof, and for increase of virtue in Christ's religion within this realm of England, and to repress and extirp all errors, heresies and other enormities and abuses heretofore used in the same, Be it enacted by authority of this present Parliament that the King our sovereign lord, his heirs and successors kings of this realm, shall be taken, accepted and reputed the only supreme head in earth of the church of England called *Anglicana Ecclesia*, and shall have and enjoy annexed and united to the imperial crown of this realm as well the title and style thereof, as all honours, dignities, preeminences, jurisdictions, privileges, authorities, immunities, profits and commodities, to the said dignity of supreme head of the same church belonging and appertaining. And that our said sovereign lord, his heirs and successors kings of this realm, shall have full power and authority from time to time to visit, repress, redress, reform, order, correct, restrain and amend all such errors, heresies, abuses, offences, contempts and enormities, whatsoever they be, which by any manner spiritual authority or jurisdiction ought or may lawfully be reformed, repressed, ordered, redressed, corrected, restrained or amended, most to the pleasure of Almighty God, the increase of virtue in Christ's religion, and for the conservation of the peace, unity and tranquillity of this realm: any usage, custom, foreign laws, foreign authority, prescription or any other thing or things to the contrary hereof notwithstanding.

(Statutes of the Realm, III, 492.)

1. Convocation had recognized Henry as Supreme Head when it agreed to submit its canons for ratification.

DOCUMENT I, ii   The first Injunctions of King Henry VIII, 1536 (extract)

One of the main practical implications of the supremacy was that it gave the king the right to conduct ecclesiastical visitations, and to issue injunctions with binding force. The first general Injunctions were issued in the king's name in 1536, Thomas Cromwell having been appointed Viceregent in Spirituals to administer them.

In the name of God, Amen. In the year of our Lord God, 1536, and of the most noble reign of our sovereign lord Henry VIII, King of England and of France, the twenty-eighth year, and the _____ day of _____, I, Thomas Crumwel, Knight, Lord Crumwel, Keeper of the privy seal of our said sovereign lord the King, and viceregent unto the same for and concerning all his jurisdiction ecclesiastical within this realm, visiting by the King's highness' supreme authority eccesiastical the people and clergy of this deanery of _____ by my trusty commissary _____ lawfully deputed and constituted for this part, have to the Glory of Almighty God, to the King's highness' honour, the public weal of this his realm, and increase of virtue in the same, appointed and assigned these injunctions ensuing, to be kept and observed of the dean, parsons, vicars, curates, and stipendiaries resident or having cure of souls, or any other spiritual administration within this deanery, under the pains hereafter limited and appointed.

1. The first is, that the dean, parsons, vicars, and others having cure of souls anywhere within this deanery, shall faithfully keep and observe, and as far as in them may lie, shall cause to be observed and kept of other, all and singular laws and statutes of this realm made for the abolishing and extirpation of the Bishop of Rome's pretensed and usurped power and jurisdiction within this realm, and for the establishment and confirmation of the King's authority and jurisdiction

within the same, as of the Supreme Head of the Church of England, and shall to the uttermost of their wit, knowledge, and learning, purely, sincerely, and without any colour of dissimulation declare, manifest and open for the space of one quarter of a year now next ensuing, once every Sunday, and after that at leastwise twice every quarter, in their sermons and other collations, that the Bishop of Rome's usurped power and jurisdiction, having no establishment nor ground by the law of God, was of most just causes taken away and abolished; and therefore they owe unto him no manner of obedience or subjection, and that the King's power is within his dominion the highest power and potentate under God, to whom all men within the same dominion by God's commandment owe most loyalty and obedience, afore and above all other powers and potentates in earth.

2. *Item*, Whereas certain Articles were lately devised and put forth by the King's highness' authority, and condescended unto by the prelates and clergy of this his realm in Convocation, whereof part are necessary to be holden and believed for our salvation, and the other part do concern and touch certain laudable ceremonies, rites and usages of the Church meet and convenient to be kept and used for a decent and politic order in the same;[1] the said dean, parsons, vicars, and other curates shall so open and declare in their said sermons and other collations the said articles unto them that be under their cure, that they may plainly show and discern which of them be necessary to be believed and observed for their salvation; and which of them be not necessary, but only do concern the decent and politic order of the said Church, according to such commandment and admonition as has been given unto them heretofore by authority of the King's highness in that behalf.

(W.H. Frere and W.M. Kennedy, *Visitation Articles and Injunctions of the Period of the Reformation*, II, 2–5.)

1. The Ten Articles of July 1536.

DOCUMENT I, iii   Royal Injunctions of King Edward VI; proclaimed 31 July 1547 (extracts)

Following his father's example, Edward VI issued Injunctions in 1547, requiring further progress in a reforming direction. There were doubts at first as to whether a king who was a minor could exercise the supremacy. These Injunctions were partly intended to answer such doubts.

The King's most Royal Majesty, by the advice of his most dear uncle, the Duke of Somerset, Lord Protector of all his realms, dominions, and subjects, and governor of his most royal person, and the residue of his most honorable council, intending the advancement of the true honor of Almighty God, the suppression of idolatry and superstition throughout all his realms and dominions, and to plant true religion, to the extirpation of all hypocrisy, enormities, and abuses, as to his duty appertaineth, doth minister unto his loving subjects these godly Injunctions hereafter following; whereof part were given unto them heretofore by the authority of his most dearly beloved father, King Henry VIII[1] of the most famous memory, and part are now ministered and given by his majesty; all which Injunctions his highness willeth and commandeth his said loving subjects, by his supreme authority, obediently to receive and truly to observe and keep, every man in their offices, degrees, and states, as they will avoid his displeasure and the pains in the same Injunctions hereafter expressed.

The first is that all deans, archdeacons, parsons, vicars, and other ecclesiastical persons shall faithfully keep and observe, and as far as in them may lie, shall cause to be observed and kept of other, all and singular laws and statutes made as well for the abolishing and extirpation of the Bishop of Rome, his pretensed and usurped power and jurisdiction, as for the establishment and confirmation of the King's authority, jurisdiction, and supremacy of the Church of England and Ireland . . .

Item, that they, the persons above rehearsed, shall make or cause to be made, in their churches and every other cure they have, one sermon every quarter of the year at the least wherein they shall purely and sincerely declare the word of God, and in the same exhort their hearers to the works of faith, mercy, and charity specially prescribed and commanded in Scripture, and that works devised by man's phantasies, besides Scripture, as wandering to pilgrimages, offering of money, candles, or tapers to relics or images, or kissing and licking of the same, praying upon beads, or such like superstition, have not only no promise of reward in Scripture for doing of them, but contrarywise, great threats and maledictions of God, for that they be things tending to idolatry and superstition, which of all other offenses God Almighty doth most detest and abhor, for that the same diminish His honor and glory . . .

Also, that they shall provide within three months next after this visitation one book of the whole Bible, of the largest volume, in English; and within one twelve months next after the said visitation the *Paraphrases*[2] of Erasmus, also in English, upon the Gospels; and the same set up in some convenient place within the said church that they have cure of, whereas their parishioners may most commodiously resort unto the same and read the same;

Also, that every dean, archdeacon, master of collegiate church, master of hospital, and prebendiary, being priest, shall preach by himself personally twice every year at the least, either in the place where he is entitled or in some church where he hath jurisdiction, or else which is to the said place appropriate or united . . .

Also, that they shall take away, utterly extinct, and destroy all shrines, covering of shrines, all tables, candlesticks, trindles or rolls of wax, pictures, paintings, and all other monuments of feigned miracles, pilgrimages, idolatry, and superstition, so that there remain no memory of the same in walls, glasses, windows, or elsewhere within their churches or houses. And they shall exhort all their parishioners to do the like within their several houses. And that the churchwardens, at the common charge of the parishioners, in every church shall provide a comely and honest pulpit to be set in a convenient place within the same, for the preaching of God's word . . .

Also, because through lack of preachers in many places of the King's realms and dominions the people continue in ignorance and blindness, all parsons, vicars, and curates shall read in their churches, every Sunday, one of the *Homilies*[3] which are and shall be set forth for the same purpose by the King's authority, in such sort as they shall be appointed to do in the preface of the same . . .

(P.L. Hughes and J.F. Larkin, *Tudor Royal Proclamations*, I, 393–403.)

1. The second Royal Injunctions of Henry VIII; Bib. 5, Vol. II, pp. 34–43; and Bib. 7, Vol. I, pp. 270–6, 16 November 1538.
2. Brief commentaries upon the Gospels, published in English translation in 1534.
3. Model sermons upon doctrinal or moral themes, for the benefit of clergy unable or unwilling to preach their own sermons. Published in 1547.

DOCUMENT I, iv The First Edwardian Act of Uniformity (extracts)

In 1549 the first uniform liturgical order was introduced for the whole country. It was largely a translation into English of the Sarum Use, and was the first protestant liturgy in England. It signalled the alteration of the doctrinal basis of the Church by means of the royal supremacy.

An Act for the uniformity of service and administration of the
sacraments throughout the realm. (2 & 3 Ed. VI, c. 1).

Where of long time there had been in this realm of England and Wales
divers forms of common prayer commonly called the service of the
Church, that is to say, the use of Sarum, of York, of Bangor and of
Lincoln; and besides the same now of late much more divers and
sundry forms and fashions have been used in the cathedral and parish
churches of England and Wales, as well concerning the matins or
morning prayer and the evensong, as also concerning the holy
communion commonly called the mass, with divers and sundry rites
and ceremonies concerning the same and in the administration of
other sacraments of the Church; and as the doers and executors of the
said rites and ceremonies in other form than of late years they have
been used were pleased therewith, so others not using the same rites
and ceremonies were thereby greatly offended; and albeit the King's
Majesty, with the advice of his most entirely beloved uncle the Lord
Protector and other of his Highness' Council, hath heretofore divers
times assayed to stay innovations or new rites concerning the
premises, yet the same hath not had such good success as his Highness
required in that behalf; whereupon his Highness by the most prudent
advice aforesaid, being pleased to bear with the frailty and weakness
of his subjects in that behalf, of his great clemency hath not been only
content to abstain from punishment of those that have offended in
that behalf, for that his Highness taketh that they did it of a good zeal,
but also to the intent a uniform, quiet and godly order should be had
concerning the premises, hath appointed the archbishop of Canterbury and certain of the most learned and discreet bishops and other
learned men of this realm to consider and ponder the premises, and
thereupon having as well eye and respect to the most sincere and pure
Christian religion taught by the Scripture as to the usages in the
primitive Church, should draw and make one convenient and meet
order, rite and fashion of common and open prayer and administration of the sacraments, to be had and used in his Majesty's realm of
England and in Wales; the which at this time, by the aid of the Holy
Ghost, with one uniform agreement is of them concluded, set forth
and delivered to his Highness, to his great comfort and quietness of
mind, in a book entitled The Book of the Common Prayer and
Administration of the Sacraments and other Rites and Ceremonies of
the Church after the Use of the Church of England . . . and that all
and singular ministers in any cathedral or parish church, or other

place within this realm of England, Wales, Calais and marches of the same, or other the King's dominions, shall from and after the feast of Pentecost next coming be bounden to say and use the matins, evensong, celebration of the Lord's Supper commonly called the mass, and administration of each of the sacraments, and all their common and open prayer, in such order and form as is mentioned in the said book and none other or otherwise.

(*Statutes of the Realm*, IV, 37.)

DOCUMENT I, v Bishop Hooper to Henry Bullinger

During his years in exile under Henry VIII, John Hooper had made many Continental friends, one of whom was Heinrich Bullinger of Zurich. Like many other Edwardian protestants, Hooper felt that his failure to evangelize effectively during Edward's reign had earned the divine scourge of Mary's accession.

Dated from prison, 3 September 1553

GREETING. You have been accustomed, my very dear gossip, heavily to complain of me, and very properly, for having so seldom written to you. But I have now written you many letters during the past year, without having received a single one in reply. I know that you are not unacquainted with the state of our kingdom. Our king has been removed from us by reason of our sins, to the very great peril of our church. His sister Mary has succeeded, whom I pray God always to aid by his Holy Spirit, that she may reign and govern in all respects to the glory of his name. The altars are again set up throughout the kingdom; private masses are frequently celebrated in many quarters; the true worship of God, true invocation, the right use of the sacraments, are all done away with; divine things are trodden under foot, and human things have the pre-eminence. May God be present with his church, for the sake of his only Son Jesus Christ! All godly preachers are placed in the greatest danger: those who have not yet known by experience the filthiness of a prison, are hourly looking for it. Meanwhile they are all of them forbidden to preach by public authority. The enemies of the gospel are appointed in their places, and proclaim to the people from the pulpit human doctrines instead of divine truths. We now place our confidence in God alone, and earnestly entreat him to comfort and strengthen us to endure any sufferings whatever for the glory of his name. In haste, from prison,

at London, Sept. 3, 1553. Salute our very dear wife,[1] masters Biblian-
der, Pellican, and Gualter, with their wives, and all the other godly
brethren; likewise my countryman master Butlere with his wife.

Yours wholly,
JOHN HOOPER, bishop of
Worcester and Gloucester

(*Original Letters Relative to the English Reformation*, ed. H. Robinson,
(Parker Society, 1846), 100–1.)

1. Anne Hooper (née De Tserclas) came from a French-speaking Strasbourg
    family. John Hooper had married her in Basle towards the end of 1546.

DOCUMENT I, vi   Directions of Queen Mary to her Council, touching the Reformation of the Church, out of her own Original

*Although Mary had formally renounced the supremacy in January 1555,
she continued to issue policy directives concerning the enforcement of the
religious reaction. This instruction to the Council gives a good indication
of her priorities.*

First, That such as had Commision to talk with my Lord Cardinal[1] at
his first coming, touching the Goods of the Church, should have
recourse unto him, at the least once in a week, not only for putting
these Matters in execution, as much as may be, before the Parliament,
but also to understand of him which way might be best to bring to
good effect, those Matters that have been begun concerning Religion.
Both touching good Preaching, I wish that may supply and overcome
the evil Preaching in time past; and also to make a sure Provision, that
no evil Books shall either be printed, bought, or sold, without just
punishment. Therefore I think it should be well done, that the Universities and Churches of this Realm, should be visited by such
Persons as my Lord Cardinal, with the rest of you, may be well
assured to be worthy and sufficient Persons to make a true and just
account thereof, remitting the choice of them to him and you.
Touching punishment of Hereticks, me thinketh it ought to be done
without rashness, not leaving in the mean while to do Justice to such,
as by Learning would seem to deceive the simple; and the rest to be
used, that the People might well perceive them not to be condemned
without just occasion, whereby they shall both understand the Truth,

and beware to do the like. And especially in *London*, I would wish none to be burnt, without some of the Councils presence, and both there and every-where, good Sermons at the same. I verily believe that many Benefices should not be in one Man's hand, but after such sort as every Priest might look to his own Charge, and remain resident there, whereby they should have but one Bond to discharge towards God; Whereas now they have many, which I take to be the cause that in most part of this Realm there is over-much want of good Preachers, and such as should with their Doctrine overcome the evil diligence of the abused Preachers in the time of Schism, not only by their Preachings, but also by their good Example, without which, in mine opinion, their Sermons shall not so much profit as I wish. And like-as their good Example, on their behalf, shall undoubtedly do much good, so I account my self bound, on my behalf also, to shew such example, in encouraging and maintaining those Persons, well-doing their Duty, (not forgetting, in the mean while, to correct and punish them which do contrary) that it may be evident to all this Realm how I discharge my Conscience therein, and minister true Justice in so doing.

(Gilbert Burnet, *History of the Reformation in England*, II, 292–3.)

1. Cardinal Reginald Pole, who had returned to England as papal legate in November 1554.

DOCUMENT I, vii Mary's Second Statute of Repeal, 1554 (1 & 2 Philip & Mary, c.8) (extract)

Mary was determined to restore not only the traditional forms of worship, but also the full jurisdiction of the catholic Church. After prolonged negotiations, she persuaded Parliament to rescind the Henrician statutes in return for being allowed to keep the secularized church lands which many gentry and others had purchased.

Whereas since the 20th year of King Henry the Eighth of famous memory, father unto your Majesty our most natural Sovereign and gracious Lady and Queen, much false and erroneous doctrine hath been taught, preached, and written, partly by divers the natural-born subjects of this realm, and partly being brought in hither from sundry other foreign countries, hath been sown and spread abroad within the same; by reason whereof as well the spiritualty as the temporalty of your Highness's realms and dominions have swerved from the obedience of the See Apostolic and declined from the unity of Christ's

Church, and so have continued, until such time as your Majesty being first raised up by God and set in the seat royal over us, and then by his divine and gracious Providence knit in marriage with the most noble and virtuous prince, the King our Sovereign Lord your husband, the Pope's Holiness and the See Apostolic sent hither unto your Majesties (as unto persons undefiled and by God's goodness preserved from the common infection aforesaid) and to the whole realm, the most Reverend Father in God the Lord Cardinal Pole, Legate *de latere*, to call us home again into the right way, from whence we have all this long while wandered and strayed abroad and we after sundry long and grievous plagues and calamities, seeing by the goodness of God our own errors, have acknowledged the same unto the said most Reverend Father, and by him have been and are the rather at the contemplation of your Majesties received and embraced into the unity and bosom of Christ's Church;[1] and upon our humble submission and promise made, for a declaration of our repentance, to repeal and abrogate such acts and statutes as had been made in Parliament since the said 20th year of the said King Henry the Eighth, against the Supremacy of the See Apostolic, as in our submission exhibited to the said most Reverend Father in God by your Majesties appeareth.

(*Statutes of the Realm*, IV, 246.)

1. Cardinal Pole had solemnly absolved the realm from schism in a session of Parliament on 30 November.

DOCUMENT I, viii   The Act of Supremacy 1559 (extract)

In spite of the reconciliation, unease about Church property continued, and when Elizabeth wished to restore the royal supremacy in 1559, the only determined opposition came from the bishops in the House of Lords.

An Act restoring to the Crown the ancient jurisdiction over the state ecclesiastical and spiritual, and abolishing all foreign power repugnant to the same (Act of Supremacy, 1559: 1 Eliz. I, c.I).

Most humbly beseeches your most excellent Majesty your faithful and obedient subjects the Lords spiritual and temporal and the Commons in this your present Parliament assembled: that where in time of the reign of your most dear father of worthy memory, King

Henry the Eighth, divers good laws and statutes were made and established, as well for the utter extinguishment and putting away of all usurped and foreign powers and authorities out of this your realm and other your Highness' dominions and countries, as also for the restoring and uniting to the imperial crown of this realm the ancient jurisdictions, authorities, superiorities and preeminences to the same of right belonging and appertaining; by reason whereof we your most humble and obedient subjects, from the five and twentieth year of the reign of your said dear father, were continually kept in good order and were disburdened of divers great and intolerable charges and exactions before that time unlawfully taken and exacted by such foreign power and authority as before that was usurped, until such time as all the said good laws and statutes by one act of Parliament made in the first and second years of the reigns of the late King Philip and Queen Mary, your Highness' sister [1 & 2 Philip and Mary, c.8], were all clearly repealed and made void, as by the same act of repeal more at large doth and may appear. By reason of which act of repeal your said humble subjects were eftsoons brought under an usurped foreign power and authority and yet do remain in that bondage, to the intolerable charges of your loving subjects if some redress by the authority of this your High Court of Parliament with the assent of your Highness be not had and provided. May it therefore please your Highness, for the repressing of the said usurped foreign power and the restoring of the rights, jurisdictions and preeminences appertaining to the imperial crown of this your realm, that it may be enacted by the authority of this present Parliament, That the said act . . . and all and every branch, clauses and articles therein contained (other than such branches, clauses and sentences as hereafter shall be excepted) may from the last day of this session of Parliament, by authority of this present Parliament, be repealed, and shall from thenceforth be utterly void and of none effect . . .

VII. And to the intent that all usurped and foreign power and authority, spiritual and temporal, may for ever be clearly extinguished and never to be used nor obeyed within this realm or any other your Majesty's dominions or countries: May it please your Highness that it may be further enacted by the authority aforesaid that no foreign prince, person, prelate, state or potentate, spiritual or temporal, shall at any timc after the last day of this session of Parliament use, enjoy or exercise any manner or power, jurisdiction, superiority, authority, pre-eminence or privilege spiritual or ecclesiastical, within this realm or within any other your Majesty's dominions or countries that now be or hereafter shall be, but from thenceforth the same shall be clearly abolished out of this realm, and all other your Highness' dominions for ever; any statute, ordinance, custom, constitutions or any other matter or cause whatsoever to the contrary in any wise notwithstanding . . .

XX. Provided always and be it enacted by the authority aforesaid that such person or persons to whom your Highness, your heirs or succesors, shall hereafter by letters patent under the great seal of England give authority to have or execute any jurisdiction, power or authority spiritual, or to visit, reform, order, or correct any errors, heresies, schisms, abuses or enormities by virtue of this act, shall not in any wise have authority or power to order, determine or adjudge any matter or cause to be heresy but only such as heretofore have been determined, ordered or adjudged to be heresy by the authority of the canonical Scriptures, or by the first four General Councils or any of them or by any other General Council within the same was declared heresy by the express and plain words of the said canonical Scriptures, or such as hereafter shall be ordered, judged or determined to be heresy by the High Court of Parliament of this realm with the assent of the clergy in their Convocation; anything in this act contained to the contrary notwithstanding.

(*Statutes of the Realm*, IV, 350–5.)

DOCUMENT I, ix   The ecclesiastical commission of 1559 (extracts)

Elizabeth, being reluctant to exercise the supremacy directly, styled herself 'Supreme Governor' rather than Supreme Head, and set up a commission, dominated by laymen, to exercise that authority on her behalf.

I. Elizabeth by the Grace of God, etc., to the reverend father in God Matthew Parker, nominated bishop of Canterbury, and Edmund Grindal, nominated bishop of London, and to our right trusted and right well-beloved councillors, Francis Knowles our vice-chamberlain and Ambrose Cave, knights, and to our trusty and well-beloved Anthony Cooke and Thomas Smith, knights, William Bill our almoner, Walter Haddon and Thomas Sackford, masters of our requests, Rowland Hill and William Chester, knights, Randall

Cholmely and John Southcote, serjeants-at-the-law, William May, doctor of law, Francis Cave, Richard Goodrich and Gilbert Gerard, esquires, Robert Weston and Thomas Huick, doctors of law, greeting.

II. Where at our parliament holden at Westminster the 25th day of January . . . there was two acts and statutes made and established[1] . . . and where divers seditious and slanderous persons do not cease daily to invent and set forth false rumours, tales and seditious slanders, not only against us and the said good laws and statutes, but also have set forth divers seditious books within this our realm of England, meaning thereby to move and procure strife, division and dissension amongst our loving and obedient subjects, much to the disquieting of us and our people.

III. Wherefore we, earnestly minding to have the same acts before mentioned to be duly put in execution, and such persons as shall hereafter offend in anything contrary to the tenor and effect of the said several statutes to be condignly punished; and having especial trust and confidence in your wisdoms and discretions, have authorised, assigned and appointed you to be our commissioners, and by these presents do give our full power and authority to you, or six of you, whereof you the said Matthew Parker, Edmund Grindal, Thomas Smith, Walter Haddon, Thomas Sackford, Richard Goodrich, and Gilbert Gerard to be one, from time to time hereafter during our pleasure to enquire as well by the oaths of twelve good and lawful men as also by witnesses and other ways and means ye can devise, for all offences, misdoers and misdemeanours done and committed, and hereafter to be committed or done, contrary to the tenor and effect of the said several acts and statutes and either of them; and also of all and singular heretical opinions, seditious books, contempts, conspiracies, false rumours, tales, seditions, misbehaviours, slanderous words or showings, published, invented or set forth . . . by any person or persons against us, or contrary or against . . . the quiet government and rule of our people and subjects, in any county, city, borough or other place of places within this our realm of England, and of all and every the coadjutors, counsellors, comforters, procurers and abettors of every such offender . . .

XVII. And we will and grant that these our letters patents shall be a sufficient warrant and discharge for you and every of you against us, our heirs and successors, and all and every other person or persons, whatsoever they be, of and for or concerning the premises or any parcel hereof, of or for the execution of this our commission or any part thereof. Witness the Queen at Westminster, the 19th day of July.

PER IPSAM REGINAM

> (G.W. Prothero, *Select Statutes and Other Constitutional Documents Illustrative of the Reigns of Elizabeth and James I*, 227–32.)

1. The Acts of Supremacy and Uniformity (1 Elizabeth, c.1 and c.2)

SECTION II: The Church as an Institution

DOCUMENT II, i   The Dissolution of the Monasteries, 1536 (extracts)

The fashion for endowing religious houses had long since come to an end, and the population of monks, friars and nuns had never recovered from the Black Death. There were good grounds for pruning the foundations; but the king, who was mainly interested in property, took a very blunt instrument to the task. All monasteries with an income of less than £200 a year were dissolved.

An Act whereby all religious houses of monks, canons and nuns which may not dispend manors, lands, tenements and hereditaments above the clear yearly value of £200 are given to the King's Highness, his heirs and successors, for ever (1536: 27 Henry VIII, c.28).

Forasmuch as manifest sin, vicious, carnal and abominable living, is daily used and committed amongst the little and small abbeys, priories and other religious houses of monks, canons and nuns, where the congregation of such religious persons is under the number of 12 persons, . . . so that without such small houses be utterly suppressed and the religious persons therein committed to great and honourable monasteries of religion in this realm, where they may be compelled to live religiously for the reformation of their lives, there can else be no reformation in this behalf: In consideration whereof the King's most royal Majesty, being supreme head in earth under God of the Church of England, daily finding and devising the increase, advancement and exaltation of true doctrine and virtue in the said Church, to the only glory and honour of God and the total extirping and destruction of vice and sin, having knowledge that the premises be true, as well by the compts of his late visitations as by sundry credible informations,

considering also that divers and great solemn monasteries of this
realm wherein, thanks be to God, religion is right well kept and
observed, be destitute of such full numbers of religious persons as
they ought and may keep, hath thought good that a plain declaration
should be made of the premises as well to the Lords spiritual and
temporal as to other his loving subjects the Commons in this present
Parliament assembled; whereupon the said Lords and Commons by
a great deliberation finally be resolved that it is and shall be much
more to the pleasure of Almighty God and for the honour of this his
realm that the possessions of such spiritual religious houses, now
being spent, spoiled and wasted for increase and maintenance of sin,
should be used and converted to better uses, and the unthrifty
religious persons so spending the same to be compelled to reform
their lives; and thereupon most humbly desire the King's Highness
that it may be enacted by authority of this present Parliament, that his
Majesty shall have and enjoy to him and to his heirs for ever all and
singular monasteries, priories and other religious houses of monks,
canons and nuns, of what kinds or diversities of habits, rules or orders
so ever they be called or named, which have not in lands and
tenements, rents, tithes, portions and other hereditaments above the
clear yearly value of two hundred pounds; and in like manner shall
have and enjoy all the sites and circuits of every such religious houses,
and all and singular the manors, granges, meses,[1] lands, tenements,
reversions, rents, services, tithes, pensions, portions, churches,
chapels, advowsons, patronages, annuities, rights, entries, conditions
and other hereditaments appertaining or belong to every such
monastery, priory or other religious house not having as is aforesaid
above the said clear yearly value of two hundred pounds, in as large
and ample manner as the abbots, priors, abbesses, prioresses or other
governors of such monasteries and other religious houses now have or
ought to have the same in the right of their houses; and that also his
Highness shall have to him and to his heirs all and singular such
monasteries, abbeys and priories which, at any time within one year
next afore the making of this act, hath been given and granted to his
Majesty by any abbot, prior, abbess or prioress under their convent
seals, or that otherwise hath been suppressed or dissolved; And all and
singular the manors, lands, [etc.] . . . to the same monasteries, abbeys
and priories or to any of them appertaining or belonging; To have and
to hold all and singular the premises with all their rights, profits,
jurisdictions and commodities, unto the King's Majesty and to his
heirs and assigns for ever, to do and use therewith his or their own

wills to the pleasure of Almighty God and to the honour and profit of this realm.

(Statutes of the Realm, III, 575–7.)

1. Houses.

DOCUMENT II, ii   Report of the surrender of the friars, Gloucester

The friaries, although many of them were poor, were not dissolved, but the pressure for reform was tantamount to an encouragement to surrender. Almost all took the hint, as in this case at Gloucester.

Memorandum, thys xxviij. day of Julii, in the xxx. yer of ower most dred soveren lord kyng Henry the viij^{te}, Richard byschop of Dowor and vesytor under the lord prevy selle[1] for the kynges grace was in Glowsetur, and ther befor the meyar and alderman in the howseys of freeres ther at ij. tymeys in ij. days putt the seyd freeres att ther lyberteys, whether they vold contynew in ther howseys and kepe ther relygyon and injuxcyons accordeyng to the same, or ellys gyff ther howseys into the kynges handdes. The injuxcyons, he ther declareyd among them, the whyche war thowthe by the seyd meyar and alderman to be good and resonabyll, and also the seyd freeres seyd that they war accordeyng to ther rewlys, yet as the warlde ys nowe they war nott abull to kepe them and leffe in ther howseys, wherfore voluntaryly they gaffe ther howseys into the vesytores handes to the kynges use. The vesytor seyd to them, "thynke not, nor hereafter reportt nott, that ye be suppresseyd, for I have noo suche auctoryte to suppresse you, but only to reforme yow, wherfor yf ye woll be reformedy accordeyng to good order, ye may contynew for all me." They seyed they war nott abull to contynew. Wherfor the vesytor toke ther howseys, and charytabully delyveryd them, and gaff them letteres to vestyte ther fryndes, and so to goo to oder howseys, with the whyche they war wery well contentt, and soo departeyd. Thys we the seyd meyar and alderman testyfy by ower handes subscrybeyd.

Maister WYLLYAM HASARD, meyr.

Maister WYLYAM MATHEW, aldermon.

Mr. THOMAS BELL the elder, alderman.

THOMAS PAYNE, alderman.

(The Suppression of the Monasteries, Camden Society, Vol. 26 (1843), 202–3.)

1. Thomas Cromwell.

DOCUMENT II, iii   A bishop's Injunctions to his cathedral clergy

The general shortage of educated and committed clerics meant that cathedrals tended to be used as 'power houses'. This was equally true of the Marian and Elizabethan regimes, so the standards of performance and conformity expected were high.

Injunctions given to the Cathedral Church at Hereford by the Right Reverend Father in God, Richard, Bishop of Worcester, Commissioner to the most Reverend Father Reginald Poole, Cardinal and Lord Legate to the King and Queen's Majesties and to the whole nation of England from the Pope's Holiness and the See Apostolical of Rome: the xxij day of July, in the year of our Lord God 1556, inviolably to be observed under the pain of contempt.

1.   *Imprimis.* All your canons and petit-canons and vicars shall avoid the company of heretics, and other lewd and defamed persons: also they shall avoid suspicious houses, often going to taverns and alehouses.

2.   *Item,* the canons, petit-canons, and vicars going into the town shall take his servant, his scholar, his fellow, or some other honest person with him, and wear decent apparel with a tippet.

3.   *Item,* the canons, petit-canons, and vicars shall not study in the choir at that time of Divine Service, nor use there any book for study, but shall apply themselves at that time to sing and pray.

4.   *Item,* none of them shall at the time of service walk in the Church, talk, jangle, or laugh in the Choir, or sit out of his place, but behave himself devoutly and reverently as that time and place do require . . .

6.   *Item,* that no woman shall be admitted to do any service to any within the precincts of this close unless it be in time of their sickness under the pain of the law.

7.   *Item,* you shall provide with as convenient speed as you can a comely tabernacle in a fair pyx to keep the Blessed Sacrament upon the high Altar or in some convenient place nigh thereunto and cause light continually to be kept burning before it . . .

11.   *Item,* on S. Andrew's day[1] in every year to come you shall keep a solemn procession for a remembrance and thanksgiving to Almighty God for the reconciliation of this Church of England from schism to

the unity of the Catholic Church, and to the Pope's Holiness, Christ's General Vicar and Supreme Head of the same Church in Earth; also on that day in Masstime, a sermon shall be made by one of the canons wherein shall be declared the cause of such procession and the great benefit of this reconciliation, or an homily made for that purpose shall be read.

(W.H. Frere and W.M. Kennedy, *Visitation Articles and Injunctions*, II, 392–6.)

1. 30 November; see above p. 86.

DOCUMENT II, iv Cardinal Pole's *Sede Vacante*[1] visitation of the diocese of Lincoln, 1556 (extract)

Although heresy plays such a large part in the story of the Marian Church, the preoccupations of the visitors to ordinary parishes were usually quite different, concentrating on misdemeanours and dilapidations.

Walton   William Cocking . . . is presented for adultery with several women; particularly with Alice Crosse. On this citation the woman has appeared and submitted to penance. The said William has not appeared (and is excommunicated for contumaciousness).

The chancel and the nave of the church are in poor repair. The rector and parishioners are to blame. They had until Easter to carry out the repairs. The rector has gone away to Manchester in Warwickshire. The case is referred to the Archdeacon of Leicester.

Barkby   Vacant

Belgrave   Vacant; they have neither rector nor vicar. The bishop of Lichfield is patron. He has been written to.

Prestwolde Vacant; they have neither rector nor vicar. The Lord Cardinal is patron . . .

Billesdon   The chancel is almost ruined, which is the fault of Mr Thomas Hasilwoode, who holds the tithes of the rectory. The graveyard is in need of repair. They lack ornaments. They had until Easter to rectify matters. It has not been certified. The case is referred to the Archdeacon of Leicester.

Norton The windows in the chancel are broken, which is the fault of Mr Turpin, who holds the tithes of the rectory. The churchyard wall needs repair; animals are getting in. They had until Easter to put matters right. It has not been certified. Process as before.

(J. Strype, *Ecclesiastical Memorials*, III, 2, 402–3.)

1. When a see was vacant the right of visitation belonged to the bishop's superior, in this case the Cardinal Legate.

DOCUMENT II, v The Lord Protector's Instructions to Preachers, 1549

Preaching was the heart and soul of protestant evangelism. There were never enough preachers, and the expectations which the ecclesiastical authorities placed upon them were consistently disappointed.

The Copy of a Letter sent to all those Preachers which the King's Majesty hath licensed to Preach, from the Lord Protector's Grace, and other of the King's Majesty's most honourable Council; the 13th day of May, in the Second Year of the Reign of our Sovereign Lord, King EDWARD the Sixth.

After our right hearty Commendations, as well for the Conservation of the quietness and good order of the King's Majesty's Subjects, as that they should not, by evil and unlearned Preachers, be brought unto Superstition, Error, or evil Doctrine, or otherwise, be made stubborn and disobedient to the King's Majesty's Godly Proceedings, his Highness, by our Advice, hath thought good to inhibit all manner of Preachers, who have not such License, as in the same Proclamation[1] is allowed, to preach, or stir the People, in open and common preachings of Sermons, by any means, that the devout and godly Homilies, might the better, in the mean while, sink into the Subjects Hearts, and be learned the sooner, the People not being tossed to and fro with seditious and contentious Preaching, while every Man, according to his Zeal, some better, some worse, goeth about to set out his own Phantasie, and to draw the People to his Opinion. Nevertheless it is not his Majesty's Mind hereby clearly to extinct the lively Teaching of the Word of God, by Sermons made after such sort, as for the time the Holy Ghost shall put into the Preacher's Mind, but that such contentious, hot, and undiscreet Preachers, should be stopped; and that they only which be chosen and elect, be discreet and sober Men, should occupy that place, which was made for Edification, and not for Destruction; for the Honour of God, and Peace and Quietness of Conscience to be set forward, not for private Glory to be advanced; to appease, to teach; to instruct the People with Humility and Patience, not to make them contentious and proud; to instil into them their Duty to their Heads and Rulers, Obedience to Laws and Orders, appointed by the Superiors who have Rule of God; not that every Man should run before their Heads hath appointed them what to do, and that every Man should chuse his own way in Religion: The which thing yet being done of some Men, and they being rather provoked thereto by certain Preachers, than dehorted from it, it was necessary to set a stay therein: And yet forasmuch as we have a great confidence and trust in you, that you will not only Preach truly and sincerely the Word of God, but also will use circumspection and moderation in your Preaching, and such Godly Wisdom as shall be necessary and most convenient for the Time and Place. We have sent unto you the King's Majesty's License to Preach, but yet with this Exhortation and Admonishment, That in no wise you do stir and provoke the People to any Alteration or Innovation, other than is already set forth by the King's Majesty's Injunctions, Homilies, and Proclamations; but contrariwise, That you do in all your Sermons exhort Men to that which is at this time more necessary; that is, to the emendation of their own Lives, to the observance of the Commandments of God, to Humility, Patience, and Obedience to their Heads and Rulers; comforting the Weak, and teaching them the right way, and to flee all old Erroneous Superstitions, as the Confidence in Pardons, Pilgrimages, Beads, Religious Images, and other such of the Bishop of *Rome's* Traditions and Superstitions, with his usurped Power; the which things be here in this Realm most justly abolished; and straitly rebuking those, who of an arrogancy and proud stiffness, will take upon them to run before they be sent, to go before the rulers, to alter and change things in Religion, without Authority, teaching them to expect and tarry the time which God hath ordained, to the revealing of all Truth, and not to seek so long blindly and hidlings after it, till they bring all Orders into contempt. It is not a private Man's duty to alter Ceremonies, to innovate Orders in the Church; nor yet it is not a Preachers part to bring that into contempt and hatred, which the Prince doth either allow, or is content to suffer. The

King's Highness, by our Advice, as a Prince most earnestly given to the true knowledge of God, and to bring up his People therein, doth not cease to labour and travel by all godly means, that his Realm might be brought and kept in a most Godly and Christian Order, who only may and ought to do it. Why should a private Man, or a Preacher, take this Royal and Kingly Office upon him; and not rather, as his Duty is, obediently follow himself, and teach likewise others to follow and observe that which is commanded. What is abolished, taken away, reformed, and commanded, it is easy to see by the Acts of Parliament, the Injunctions, Proclamations and Homilies: the which things most earnestly it behoveth all Preachers in their Sermons to confirm and approve accordingly, in other things which be not yet touched, it behoveth him to think, that either the Prince doth allow them, or else suffer them; and in those it is the part of a Godly Man, not to think himself wiser than the King's Majesty, and his Council: but patiently to expect and to conform himself thereto, and not to intermeddle further to the disturbance of a Realm the disquieting of the King's People, the troubling of Mens Consciences, and disorder of the King's Subjects.

These things we have thought good to admonish you of at this time, because we think you will set the same so forward in your preaching, and so instruct the King's Majesty's People accordingly, to the most advancement of the Glory of God, and the King's Majesty's most Godly Proceedings, that we do not doubt but much profit shall ensue thereby, and great conformity in the People the which you do instruct; and so we pray you not to fail to do: and having a special regard to the weakness of the People what they may bear, and what is most convenient for the time; in no case to intermeddle in your Sermons, or otherwise, with Matters in contention or controversion, except it be to reduce the People in them also to Obedience, and following of such Orders as the King's Majesty hath already set forth, and no others, as the King's Majesty and our Trust is in you, and as you tender his Highness Will and Pleasure, and will answer to the contrary at your Peril.

Fare you well.

(G. Burnet, *History of the Reformation*, II, 130–3.)

1. Proclamation of 25 April 1548. Bib. 7, pp. 421–3.

SECTION III: The Theological Revolution

DOCUMENT III, i   John Colet's sermon to Convocation, 1511 (extracts)

Concern about the conduct and commitment of the clergy was not confined to Lollards and other dissidents. Well before the appearance of protestantism, earnest and learned reformers such as John Colet were urging the need for new attitudes and higher standards.

Wherefore I came hither today, . . . to exhort you, reverend fathers, to the endeavour of reformation of the church's estate, (because that nothing hath so disfigured the face of the Church as hath the fashion of secular and worldly living in clerks and priests) I know not where more conveniently to take beginning of my tale than of the apostle Paul, in whose temple ye are gathered together.[1] For he, writing unto the Romans, and under their name unto you, saith: *Be you not conformed to this world, but be you reformed in the newness of your understanding; that ye may prove what is the goodwill of God, well pleasing and perfect.* This did the apostle write to all Christian men, but most chiefly unto priests and bishops. Priests and bishops are the light of the world. For unto them said our Saviour: *You are the light of the world.* And he said also: *If the light that is in thee be darkness, how dark shall the darkness be?* That is to say, if priests and bishops, that should be as lights, run in the dark way of the world, how dark then shall the secular people be? Wherefore Saint Paul said chiefly unto priests and bishops: *Be you not conformable to this world, but be ye reformed.*

In the which words the apostle doeth two things. First, he doth forbid that we be not conformable to the world and be made carnal. Furthermore he doth command that we be reformed in the spirit of God, whereby we are spiritual.

. . . And first for to speak of pride of life: how much greediness and appetite of honour and dignity is nowadays in men of the Church? How run they, yea, almost out of breath, from one benefice to another; from the less to the more, from the lower to the higher?

. . . The second secular evil is carnal concupiscence. Hath not this vice so grown and waxen in the Church as a flood of their lust, so that there is nothing looked for more diligently in this most busy time of the most part of priests than that that doth delight and please the senses? They give themselves to feasts and banqueting; they spend themselves in vain babbling; they give themselves to sports and plays; they apply themselves to hunting and hawking; they drown themselves in the delights of this world.

. . . Covetousness is the third secular evil, the which Saint John the apostle calleth concupiscence of the eyes. Saint Paul calleth it idolatry. This abominable pestilence hath so entered in the mind almost of all priests, and so hath blinded the eyes of the mind, that we are blind to all things but only unto those which seem to bring unto us some gains. For what other thing seek we nowadays in the Church than fat benefices and high promotions?

. . . What should I rehearse the rest? To be short, and to conclude at one word: all corruptness, all the decay of the Church, all the offences of the world, come of the covetousness of priests; according to that of Saint Paul, that here I repeat again and beat into your ears: *covetousness is the root of all evil.*

The fourth secular evil that spotteth and maketh ill favoured the face of the church, is the continual secular occupation, wherein priests and bishops nowadays doth busy themselves, the servants rather of men than of God; the warriors rather of this world than of Christ.

. . . The second thing that Saint Paul commandeth, is that we be reformed into a new understanding; that we smell those things that be of God.

. . . This reformation and restoring of the Church's estate must needs begin of you our fathers, and so follow in us your priests and in all the clergy. You are our heads, you are an example of living unto us. Unto you we look as unto marks of our direction. In you and in your life we desire to read, as in lively books, how and after what fashion we may live. Wherefore, if you will ponder and look upon our motes, first take away the blocks out of your eyes. It is an old proverb: *Physician, heal thyself.* You spiritual physicians, first taste you this medicine of purgation of manners, and then after offer us the same to taste.

(*English Historical Documents, 1485–1558*, ed. C.H. Williams, 652–9)

1. St Paul's Cathedral.

DOCUMENT III, ii   William Tyndale, *The Obedience of a Christian Man,* 1528 (extract)

The early protestants were very keen to locate ecclesiastical authority anywhere other than in Rome. Following Luther, they tended to advocate both the sole authority of scripture and the role of the Godly Prince, without perceiving the potential contradictions between them.

That thou mayest perceive how that the Scripture ought to be in the mother tongue, and that the reasons which our spirits make for the contrary are but sophistry and false wiles to fear thee from the light, that thou mightest follow them blindfold and be their captive to honour their ceremonies and to offer to their belly: first, God gave the children of Israel a law by the hand of Moses in their mother tongue, and all the prophets wrote in their mother tongue, and all the psalms were in the mother tongue. And there was Christ but figured and described in ceremonies, in riddles, in parables and in dark prophecies. What is the cause that we may not have the Old Testament with the New also, which is the light of the Old, and wherein is openly declared before the eyes that which there was darkly prophesied? I can imagine no cause verily, except it be that we should not see the work of Antichrist and juggling of hypocrites . . .

They will say haply, 'The Scripture requireth a pure mind and a quiet mind: and therefore the layman, because he is altogether cumbered with worldly business, cannot understand them.' If that be the cause, then it is a plain case that our prelates understand not the Scriptures themselves: for no layman is so tangled with worldly business as they are. The great things of the world are ministered by them; neither do the lay people any great thing but at their assignment.

'If the Scripture were in the mother tongue', they will say, 'then would the lay people understand it every man after his own ways.' Wherefore serveth the curate but to teach him the right way? . . . Are ye not abominable schoolmasters in that ye take so great wages, if ye will not teach? If ye would teach, how could ye do it so well and with so great profit as when the lay people have the Scripture before them in their mother tongue? For then should they see, by the order of the text, whether thou jugglest or not. And then would they believe it because it is the Scripture of God, though thy living be never so abominable . . . But alas, the curates themselves (for the most part) wot no more what the New or Old Testament meaneth than do the Turks. Neither know they of any more than that they read at mass, matins and evensong, which yet they understand not . . . If they will not let the layman have the word of God in his mother tongue, yet let the priests have it; which, for a great part of them, do understand no

Latin at all; but sing and say and patter all day with the lips only that which the heart understandeth not.

(*Doctrinal Treatises*, ed. H. Walker (Parker Society, 1848), 144–6.)

DOCUMENT III, iii   William Tyndale, *Prologue to Romans*, in the revised New Testament, 1534

The central and distinguishing protestant doctrine was justification by faith alone, which removed the need for the traditional apparatus of sacramental and works salvation. To the traditional clergy this was not only blasphemous, it threatened them with redundancy.

Faith is not man's opinion and dream, as some imagine and feign when they hear the story of the gospel . . . But right faith is a thing wrought by the Holy Ghost in us, which changeth us, turneth us into a new nature and begetteth us anew in God, and maketh us the sons of God, as thou readest in the first of *John*, and killeth the old Adam and maketh us altogether new in the heart, mind, will, lust and in all our affections and powers of the soul and bringeth the Holy Ghost with her. Faith is a living thing, mighty in working, valiant and strong, ever doing, ever fruitful, so that it is impossible that he which is endued therewith should not work all ways good works without ceasing. He asketh not whether good works are to be done or not, but hath done them already ere mention be made of them, and is always doing, for such is his nature now: quick faith in his heart and lively moving of the Spirit drive him and steer him thereunto. Whosoever doeth not good works is an unbelieving person and faithless, and looketh round about groping after faith and good works, and wot not what faith or good works means, though he babble never so many things of faith and good works. Faith is then a lively and steadfast trust in the favour of God, wherewith we commit ourselves altogether unto God, and that trust is so surely grounded and sticketh so fast in our hearts, that a man would not once doubt of it, though he should die a thousand times therefore. And such trust wrought by the Holy Ghost through faith maketh a man glad, lusty, cheerful and true-hearted unto God and to all creatures. By the means whereof, willingly and without compulsion he is glad and ready to do good to every man, to do service to every man, to suffer all things, that God may be loved and praised, which hath given him such grace; so that it is impossible to separate good works from faith, even as it is impossible to separate heat and burning from fire . . .

Now go to, reader; and according to the order of Paul's writing, even so do thou.

Farewell

W.T.

(*The New Testament translated by William Tyndale*, 1534 (Cambridge University Press Reprint, 1938, 293–318).)

DOCUMENT III, iv   Queries put concerning some abuses of the mass; with the answers that were made by many bishops and divines, 1548

The mass was the principal sacrament of the traditional Church, involving both the transformation of the bread and wine into the body and blood of Christ (transubstantiation) and also the repeated offering of the sacrifice of Christ. The reformers denied both concepts, insisting that the essence of the rite was a sacramental meal (communion) in which the presence of Christ was spiritual.

What is the Oblation and Sacrifice of Christ in the Mass?

Answers.

Centaurien.[1]   The Oblation and Sacrifice of Christ in the Mass is not so called, because Christ indeed is there offered and sacrificed by the Priest and the People, (for that was done but once by himself upon the Cross) but it is so called, because it is a Memory and Representation of that very true Sacrifice and Immolation which before was made upon the Cross.

Eboracen.   The Oblation and Sacrifice of Christ in the Mass, is the presenting of the very Body and Blood of Christ to the

Heavenly Father, under the Forms of Bread and Wine, consecrated in the Remembrance of his Passion, with Prayer and Thanksgiving for the Universal Church.

London.
Worcester.
Hereford.
Norvicen.
Cicestren.
Assaven.

I think it is the Presentation of the very Body and Blood of Christ being really present in the Sacrament; which Presentation the Priest maketh at the Mass, in the Name of the Church, unto God the Father in memory of Christ's Passion and Death upon the Cross; with thanksgiving therefore, and devout Prayer, that all Christian People, and namely they which spiritually join with the Priest in the said Oblation, and of whom he maketh special remembrance, may attain the benefit of the said Passion.

Dunelm.

The Oblation and Sacrifice of Christ in the Mass, is the presenting of Christ by the Priest, in commemoration of his Passion, being our eternal and permanent Sacrifice, present in the Sacrament by his Omnipotent Word left to us, to have his Death and Passion in remembrance, with giving thanks for the same, and Prayer of the Minister, and them which be present, that the same may be available to the whole Church of Christ, both Quick and Dead in the Faith of Christ.

Which Oblation, commemoration of Christ's Passion, giving of Thanks and Prayer, taketh effect only in them which by their own proper Faith shall receive the same effect.

Sarisburie.

There is properly no Oblation nor   Lincoln.
Sacrifice, but a remembrance of the One
Oblation of Christ upon the Cross,
made once for all; a giving of Thanks for
the same, and the Prayer of the publick
Minister for the whole Congregation;
which Prayer only taketh effect in them,
who by their own proper Faith receive
the benefit of Christ: And where many
of those Authors do say there is an
Oblation and Sacrifice, they spoke to,
because in this Sacrament we be ad-
monished of the Oblation and Sacrifice
of Christ upon the Cross.

(**G.** Burnet, *History of the Reformation*, II, 136.)

1. Canterbury: Thomas Cranmer
   York: Robert Holgate
   London: Edmund Bonner
   Worcester: Nicholas Heath
   Hereford: John Skip
   Norwich: William Repps
   Chichester: George Day
   St Asaph: Robert Warton
   Durham: Cuthbert Tunstall
   Salisbury: John Salcot
   Lincoln: Henry Holbeach

Cranmer, Salcot and Holbeach express a reformed point of view; Tunstall
a conservative one; the others are hedging.

DOCUMENT III, v   The Forty-two Articles of 1553
(extracts)

*The first formal definition of the faith of the Anglican Church was
contained in the Forty-two Articles, issued just before Edward's death.
(The passages in parenthesis represent the changes and additions introduced in 1563.)*

V. *The Doctrine of the Holy Scripture is sufficient to Salvation*

(Holy scripture containeth all things necessary to Salvation, so that whatsoever is not read therein, nor may be proved thereby, is not to be required of any Man that it should be believed as an Article of the Faith, or be thought necessary or requisite to Salvation.

In the name of the Holy Scripture we do understand those Canonical Books of the Old and New Testament, of whose Authority was never any doubt in the church; that is to say, Genesis, Exodus, Leviticus, Numbers, Deuteronomy, Joshua, Judges, Ruth, 1st of Samuel, 2d of Samuel, &c. *And the Other Books (as Hierom saith) the Church doth read for example of Life, and instruction of Manners, but yet doth it not apply them to establish any Doctrine; such as these following,* The 3d of *Esdras,* the 4th of *Esdras,* the book of *Tobias,* the Book of *Judeth,* the rest of the Book of *Hester,* the Book of *Wisdom,* &c. *All the Books of the New Testament, as they are commonly received, we do receive and account them Canonical.*)

Holy Scripture containeth all things necessary to Salvation; for that whatsoever is not read therein, nor may be proved thereby, *although sometimes it may be admitted by God's faithful People as pious, and conducing unto order and decency;* yet is not to be required of any Man that it should be believed as an Article of the Faith, or be thought requisite or necessary to Salvation.

XI. *Of the Justification of Man*

Justification by Faith only in Jesus Christ, in that sense wherein it is set forth in the Homily of *Justification,* is the most certain and most wholesome Doctrine for a Christian Man.

(We are accounted Righteous before God only, for the merit of our Lord and Saviour Jesus Christ by Faith, and not for our own Works or deservings. Wherefore that we are justified by Faith, is a most wholesome Doctrine, and very full of comfort, as more largely is expressed in the Homily of *Justification.*)

(XII. *Of Good Works.*
Albeit the Good Works, which are the Fruits of Faith, and follow after Justification, cannot put

away our Sins, and endure the severity of God's Judgment, yet are they pleasing and acceptable unto God in Christ, and do spring out necessarily of a true and lively Faith, insomuch that by them, a lively Faith may be as evidently known, as a Tree discerned by the fruit.)

XII. *Works before Justification*

Works done before the Grace of Christ, and the inspiration of his Spirit, are not pleasant to God, forasmuch as they spring not of Faith in Jesus Christ; neither do they make Men meet to receive Grace, or (as the School Authors say) deserve Grace of Congruity; yea rather for that they are not done as God hath willed and commanded them to be done, we doubt not but they have the nature of Sin.

XVII. *Of Predestination and Election*

Predestination unto Life, is the everlasting Purpose of God, whereby (before the Foundations of the World were laid) he hath constantly decreed by his Counsel, secret unto us, to deliver from Curse and Damnation, those whom he hath chosen out of Man-kind, and to bring them by Christ to everlasting Salvation, as Vessels made to Honour. Wherefore they which be endued with so excellent a benefit of God, be called according to God's Purpose, by his Spirit working in due season, they through Grace obey the Calling, they be justified freely, they are made Sons of Adoption, they are made like the Image of the only begotten Jesus Christ; they walk religiously in good Works, and at length, by God's Mercy, they attain to everlasting felicity.

As the godly consideration of Predestination and Election in Christ, is full of sweet, pleasant, and unspeakable comfort to godly Persons, and such as feel in themselves the working of the Spirit of Christ, mortifying the Works of the Flesh, and their Earthly members, and drawing up their mind to high and heavenly Things, as well because it doth greatly establish and confirm their Faith of eternal Salvation, to be enjoyed through Christ, as because it doth fervently kindle their love towards God: So for curious and carnal Persons, lacking the Spirit of Christ, to have continually before their eyes the sentence of God's Predestination, is a most dangerous downfall, whereby the Devil doth thrust them either into desparation, or into wrecklessness of most unclean living, no less perilous than desparation.

Furthermore, *though the Decrees of Predestination be unknown to us, yet* must we receive God's Promises in such wise as they be generally set forth to us in Holy Scripture; and in our doings, that Will of God is to be followed, which we have expressly declared unto us in the word of God.

XX. *Of the Church*

The Visible Church of Christ, is a Congregation of faithful Men, in which the pure Word of God is preached, and the Sacraments be duly ministred, according to Christ's Ordinance, in all those things that of necessity are requisite to the same.

As the Church of *Jerusalem, Alexandria,* and *Antioch* have erred, so also the Church of *Rome* hath erred, not only in their Livings, and manner of ceremonies, but also in Matters of Faith.

XXI. *Of the Authority of the Church*

(*The Church hath power to decree Rites and Ceremonies, and Authority in Controversies of Faith.* It is not lawful for the Church, *&c.*) It is not lawful for the Church to ordain any thing that is contrary to God's Word written, neither may it so expound one place of Scripture, that it be repugnant to another; Wherefore although the Church be a Witness and Keeper of Holy Writ, yet as it ought not to decree any thing against the same, so besides the same ought it not to enforce any thing to be believed, for necessity of Salvation.

(G. Burnet, *History of the Reformation,* II, ii, 210–12.)

SECTION IV: The Faith of the People

DOCUMENT IV, i   A Lollard view

The Lollards (as the followers of John Wycliffe, the fourteenth-century Oxford master, were called) were bitterly opposed to many of the formalities and outward symbols of the catholic faith. One of their principal hatreds was the veneration of images, and the attribution of virtue to them, which the Lollards termed idolatry.

'The second trap of the fiend is called pilgrimage.'

The painter maketh an image forged with diverse colours till it seems in the eyes of fools like a living creature. This is set in the church in a solemn place, bound fast with bonds, for it should not fall. Priests of the temple beguile the people with the foul sin of Balaam[1] in their open preaching. They say that God's power in working of his miracles descends into one image more than another, and therefore 'Come and offer to this, for here is showed much virtue'. Lord, how dare these fiends for dread thus blaspheme their God and use the sin of Balaam that God's law hath damned, since Christ and his saints forsook this world's wealth and lived a poor life, as our belief teaches. Why gather riches, you priests, by your painted images, to make yourselves worldly riches in spoiling of the people?

(From *The Lantern of Light*, ed. L.M. Swinburn (Early English Text Society O.S., 151, 1917), 41.)

1. Balaam was a seer, called upon by the king of Moab to curse the Israelites, but in the New Testament he is used as a type of false prophet, one who led the Israelites into error. Here the reference appears to be to idolatry.

DOCUMENT IV, ii   A conservative view of the Edwardian changes

Traditional ceremonies were deeply rooted in the social life of parish communities, and the reformers' attempts to create a more spiritual and individual faith were seen as betraying an essential element in the relationship between the community and God.

Immediattlye followyde a grett parliamentt holden att Westminster and begonne the 23 day of January and then continewyde and keptt unto the 15 day of Aprill in the sixtt yeare of the Kings Majestie his reigne, and in the years of Our Lorde God 1552, wherin no goodnes towards holly churche proceadyde, butt all thinges contrarie. For in the parliamentt was depoisside by actt thes thre holly days before accustommyde to have been keptt holly, vz. Conversion of S. Paull, S. Barnabe & Marie Magdalen;[1] and thatt a new Comunion Boyke in Englishe (callide the Boyke of Common Prayer) sholde tayke effectt att All Hallows Day nextt ensewygne daytte hereof (vz. first day of Novembre), and so the Communion Boyke in Englische (wiche is above mentionyde) to be of none effectt. Hoo, notte the grett instabilitie and newfanglenes of therityke Warwyke (alias Duce of Northumberlande) withe his adherentts, vz. carnall byschopps of this realme

and veray tratowres to God. For consequenttlye after thatt Robertt
Hollegaytte Archebischoppe of Yorke was cum from the saide parliamentt, he sentt straitte commandementt in begyninge of Junii
through all his diocesse that the table in the qweare wher uppon tholly
Communion was ministride, itt stondynge withe thendes towarde
sowthe and northe, sholde be uside contrarie, vz. to be sett in the
qweare by neathe the lowest stare or grace, havings thendes therof
towards the east and west, and the preast his face towardes the northe
all the Communion tyme, wich was nothinge semynge nor after any
good ordre.

Item, itt was commandyde thatt no organs sholde be uside in the
church, wherby any melodie sholde be maide to Gods his honowr,
laude & praysse, butt utterly forbodden.

The tyme proceadynge, with all cruellnes thatt of heretykes cowlde
by ymaginede, itt came to passe in the monethe of August and
Septembre (anno ubi supra) thatt all parsons, vicars, curetts &
churche wardons was straittlie commandyde to gyve in trew inven-
tories indentide of all the churches' goodes, as leade, belles, chalices,
playtte and other ornamenttes unto the Kyng's Majestie his commis-
sioneres apponttide for the sayme, in lyke maner as is above saide (vz.
anno Domini 1548 ac anno Regis Edwardii sexti tertio), not yitt
certanly knowynge whatt wolde cum therof.[2]

(Extract from 'Robert Parkyn's narrative of the Reformation', ed. A.G.
Dickens, *English Historical Review*, LXII (1947), 74–5.)

1. Conversion of St Paul, 25 January; St Barnabas, 11 June; St Mary
   Magdalene, 22 July.
2. An instruction was sent out on 3 March 1551 'to take into the king's hands
   such church plate as remaineth, to be employed to his highness's use'.

DOCUMENT IV, iii   Religious dispute in southern England (Extracts from the autobiography of Thomas Hancock)

*The well-intentioned efforts of the reformers were often resisted by civic
or communal leaders, who made their disapproval clear in a variety of
demonstrations and threats.*

The first year of the reign of King Edward VI, I the said Thomas,
having licence of Bishop Cranmer, preached at Christchurch
Twinham [Hampshire], where I was born, Mr Smythe, vicar of

Christchurch and bachelor of divinity being present; where I, taking my place out of the 16 *St John*, v. 8, [said] . . . Here doth our Saviour Christ say that he goeth to the Father and that we shall see him no more. The priest being then at mass, I declared unto the people that [what] the priest doth hold over his head [the consecrated bread and wine] they did see with their bodily eyes, but our Saviour Christ doth here say plainly that we shall see him no more. Then you that do kneel unto it, pray unto it and honour it as God, do make an idol of it, and yourselves do commit most horrible idolatry. Whereat the said vicar, Mr Smythe, sitting in his chair in the face of the pulpit, spake these words, 'Mr Hancock, you have done well until now and now have you played an ill cow's part, which when she hath given a good mess of milk, overthroweth all with her foot, and so all is lost', and with these words he got him out of the church . . .

I being minister of God's word in that town of Poole, preaching the word upon some Sunday in the month of July, inveighed against Idolatry and covetousness, taking my place out of the 6th of *Timothy* . . . The brightness of the Godhead is such that it passeth the brightness of the sun, of angels and all creatures, so that it cannot be seen with our bodily eyes, for no man hath seen God at any time and liveth. The priest at that time being at mass, if it be so that no man hath seen God, nor can see God with these bodily eyes, then that which the priest lifteth over his head is not God, for you do see it with your bodily eyes: if it be not God, you may not honour it as God, neither for God. Whereat old Thomas Whyte, a great rich merchant and a ringleader of the papists, rose out of his seat and went out of the church, saying, 'Come from him, good people; he came from the devil and teacheth unto you devilish doctrine.' John Notherel, alias John Spicer, followed him, saying, 'It shall be God when thou shalt be but a knave.'

> (*Narratives of the Days of the Reformation*, ed. J.G. Nichols (*Camden Society*, Old Series, lxxvii, 1859), pp. 72–8.)

DOCUMENT IV, iv   The trial of a protestant

Not all protestants were educated men or women, but their knowledge of the Bible gave them a remarkable self-assurance — not to say obstinacy — under examination.

The martydom of Roger Coo, of Melford in Suffolk Shearman; first examined before Hopton the Bishop of Norwich, and by him condemned, August 12, anno 1555.

Roger Coo, being brought before the bishop, first was asked why he was imprisoned.

Coo: 'At the justice's commandment.'
Bishop: 'There was some cause why.'
Coo: 'Here is my accuser; let him declare.'

And his accuser said, that he would not receive the sacrament. Then the bishop said, that he thought he had transgressed a law. But Coo answered that there was no law to transgress.

The bishop then asked, what he said to the law that then was? He answered how he had been in prison a long time, and knew it not.

'No,' said his accuser, 'nor will not. My lord, ask him when he received the sacrament.'

When Coo heard him say so, he said, 'I pray you, my lord, let him sit down and examine me himself.'

But the bishop would not hear that, but said 'Coo, why? will ye not receive?'

Coo answered him, that the bishop of Rome had changed God's ordinances, and given the people bread and wine, instead of the gospel and the belief of the same.

Bishop: 'How prove you that?'
Coo: 'Our saviour said, "My flesh is meat indeed, and my blood is drink indeed. He that eateth my flesh, and drinketh my blood, abideth in me, and I in him;" and the bread and wine doth not so.'

Bishop: 'Well, Coo, thou dost slander our holy fathers. Did not Christ take bread, give thanks, and break it, and say, "This is my body?"'

'Yes', said Coo, and so he went further with the text, saying, 'Which shall be given for you: do this in remembrance of me.'

Bishop: 'You have said the truth.'

Then Coo replied further, and said, 'Christ willed to do this in remembrance of him, and not to say this in remembrance of him, neither did the Holy Ghost so lead the apostles, but taught them to give thanks, and to break bread from house to house, and not to say as the bishop said.'

Bishop: 'How prove you that?'
Coo: 'It is written in the second of the Acts.'

Then the bishop's chaplain said, it was true.

The bishop asked him if he could say his belief.

Coo answered, 'Yea,' and so said part of the creed, and then after he said, he believed more; for he believed the Ten Commandments, that it was meet for all such as look to be saved, to be obedient unto them.

Bishop: 'Is not the holy church to be believed also?'

Coo: 'Yes, if it be builded upon the word of God.'

The bishop said to Coo, that he had charge of his soul.

Coo: 'Have ye so, my lord? Then if *ye* go to the devil for your sins, where shall *I* become?'

Bishop: 'Do you not believe as your father did? Was not he an honest man?'

Coo: 'It is written, that after Christ hath suffered, "there shall come a people with the prince, that shall destroy both city and sanctuary." I pray you show me whether this destruction was in my father's time, or now?'

The bishop not answering his question, asked him whether he would not obey the king's laws.

Coo: 'As far as they agree with the word of God, I will obey them.'

Bishop: 'Whether they agree with the word of God or not, we be bound to obey them, if the king were an infidel.'

Coo: 'If Shadrach, Meshech, and Abednego had so done, Nebuchadnezzar had not confessed the living God.'

Then the bishop told him, that these twenty-two years we have been governed with such kings.

Coo: 'My lord, why were ye then dumb, and did not speak or bark?'

Bishop: 'I durst not for fear of death.'

And thus they ended. But after this done, it was reported that I railed; wherefore I called it to memory, and wrote this my railing, that light should not be taken for darkness, nor sin for holiness, and the devil for God, who ought to be feared and honoured both now and ever! Amen.

This Roger Coo, an aged father, after his sundry troubles and conflicts with his adversaries, at length was committed to the fire at Yoxford, in the county of Suffolk, where he most blessedly ended his aged years, AD 1555, in the month of September.

(John Foxe, *Acts and Monuments of the English Martyrs*, ed. S.R. Cattley and G. Townsend (1838), VII, 381–2.)

DOCUMENT IV, v   Oswestry Parish Register, November 1558

Parish registers had been introduced in 1541 to record baptisms,

marriages and burials. Resented at first as a device to facilitate taxation,
they were soon accepted as a routine aspect of parish life, and are useful
documents for the social historian.

(Written on the parchment fly leaf.)
    The feare of the lord is the beginnynge of wisdom.
    Timor d'm odit malum,
    Timor d'm'ni odit malum,
    The feare of the lord is the beginnynge of wisdom.

    Such as thou art such a one was I,
    Cut of by death loe here I lie,
    Such as I am such shalt thou be,
    Who when I lived was like to thee.

(On the third page, partly indecipherable.)
    A true and p'fect regester of (Christenings, Weddings, &)
    Burials that hath bene
    Since the seventeenth day of (November, in the first)
    Yeare of the Raigne of our (Lady Elizabeth)
    By the grace of god of England, ffraunce (& Ireland)
    Queene, deff' of the faith, &c. Anno Dm'ni. 1558
                November, 1558.
    Richard ap Owen, cristned the xixth daye.
    Katheringe vz Richard, cristned the same daye.
    Jevan ap David guttyn, buried the xxiijth daye.
    Richard ap Roger, cristned the xxiiijth daye.
    Robert ap Llew'n, maried Margret Mathewe the xxvith daye.
    Elnor vz Edward, cristned the same daye.
    Douse vz Jevan, cristned the xxixth daye.
    Katheringe vz Edward, buried the last daye.
                December, 1558
    William (blank) buried the vjth daye.
    Humffrey ap lewys and Thomas Kyffin sherma', buried the vijth
    daye.
    Richard ap Owen, cristned the same daye.
    John ap Thomas, buried the ixth daye.
    John ap lawrence, cristned the xth daye.
    Jane vz Thomas, & Richard ap Owen, buried the xjth daye
    Gryffyth ap David, buried the xiijth daye.
    M'gret vz John, buried the xiiijth daye.
    Elnor vz David, cristned the xvjth daye.

Gwenhwyfar vz Jevan, & yngharad vz hughe, buried the xviijth daye.

M'gret vz David, buried the xxjth daye.

Owen ap William, buried the xxiiijth daye.

Gwenhwyfar vz David, cristned the xxvth daye.

John ap Jevan, buried the same daye.

Shonet vz Owen, cristned the xxvith daye.

William ap David ap Roger, buried the xxvijth daye.

Alson vz John v Shonet vz John, buried the xxvijth daye.

Gwen vz John, buried the xxixth daye.

Mauld vz William, cristned the same daye.

Edward Drap' buried the last daye.

(*Shropshire Parish Registers*: Diocese of St Asaph, Vol. IV, pp. 1–2.)

SECTION V: Continental Influences

DOCUMENT V, i Luther's 'Breakthrough' from the 'Autobiographical Fragment', March 1545

Martin Luther was the founding father of protestantism. It was his concept of faith as a liberation from the burden of sin which gave the entire Reformation its essential doctrinal impetus.

For my case was this: however irreproachable my life as a monk, I felt myself in the presence of God [*coram Deo*] to be a sinner with a most unquiet conscience, nor could I believe him to be appeased by the satisfaction I could offer. I did not love — nay, I hated this just God who punishes sinners, and if not with silent blasphemy, at least with huge murmuring I was indignant against God, as if it were really not enough that miserable sinners, eternally ruined by original sin, should be crushed with every kind of calamity through the law of the Ten Commandments, but that God through the Gospel must add sorrow to sorrow, and even through the Gospel bring his righteousness and wrath to bear on us. And so I raged with a savage and confounded conscience; yet I knocked importunely at Paul in this place, with a parched and burning desire to know what he could mean.

At last, as I meditated day and night, God showed mercy and I turned my attention to the connection of the words, namely — 'The righteousness of God is revealed, as it is written: the righteous shall live by faith' — and there I began to understand that the righteousness of God is the righteousness in which a just man lives by the gift of God, in other words by faith, and that what Paul means is this: the righteousness of God, revealed in the Gospel, is *passive*, in other words that by which the merciful God justifies us through faith, as it is written, 'The righteous shall live by faith.' At this I felt myself straightway born afresh and to have entered through the open gate into paradise itself. There and then the whole face of scripture was changed; I ran through the scriptures as memory served, and collected the same analogy in other words, for example *opus Dei*, that which God works in us; *virtus Dei*, that by which God makes us strong; *sapientia Dei*, that by which He makes us wise; *fortitudo Dei*, *salus Dei*, *gloria Dei*.

(E.G. Rupp and B. Drewry, Martin Luther, 5–6.)

DOCUMENT V, ii   The presence of the body of Christ in the supper

Ulrich Zwingli was in many ways a more radical reformer than Luther. Not only did he sweep away the apparatus of works salvation, but also removed the sacramental content from the communion, something which Luther had retained.

The second thing which I have undertaken to expound at this point is this, that in the Lord's Supper the natural and essential body of Christ in which he suffered and is now seated in heaven at the right hand of God is not eaten naturally and literally but only spiritually, and that the papist teaching that the body of Christ is eaten in the same form and with the same properties and nature as when he was born and suffered and died is not only presumptuous and foolish but impious and blasphemous.

First, it is quite certain that Christ became a true man consisting of body and soul and in all points like as we are except for the propensity to sin. Hence it follows that all the endowments and properties which belong to our physical nature were most truly present in his body. For what he assumed for our sake derives from what is ours, so that he is altogether ours, as we have explained already. But if this is the case it follows indisputably, first, that the properties of our bodies belong also to his body, and second, that the properties of Christ's body are also peculiar to our bodies. For if his body possessed something physical which is lacking to ours, it would at once give rise to the impression that he had not assumed it for our sake. But why then did he assume it? For in the whole realm of the physical only man is capable of eternal blessedness.

That is why we mentioned earlier that Paul proves our own resurrection by Christ's and Christ's by ours. For when he says: 'If the dead rise not, then is Christ not raised,' how else can his argument be valid? For since Christ is both God and man, it might be objected at once: You are beside yourself, theologian. For Christ's body can and must rise again, being conjoined with his divinity. But our bodies are not able to rise again, because they are not united with God. But Paul's argument is valid for this reason, that whatever nature and endowments and properties the body of Christ may have, it has as an archetype for us. Hence it follows: Christ's body rose again, therefore our bodies shall rise. We rise again, therefore Christ is risen.

It was from these courses that that pillar of theologians, Augustine, drew when he said that the body of Christ has to be in some particular place in heaven by reason of its character as a true body. And again: Seeing that the body of Christ rose from the dead, it is necessarily in one place. The body of Christ is not in several places at one and the same time any more than our bodies are. This is not our view, but that of the apostles and Augustine and the faith in general: for even if we had no witnesses to it, it would be proved by the fact that Christ became in all points like as we are. For our sake he took to himself human frailty and was found in fashion as a man, that is, in endowments, attributes and properties. In this way, most excellent king, I believe that incidentally I will have made it plain to you with what injustice we are branded as heretics in respect of the sacrament of the Lord's Supper, although we never taught a single word that we have not taken from Holy Scripture or the Fathers.

(*Zwingli Opera*, ed. Schuler and Schultess, IV, 74ff.: English text from the Library of Christian Classics, Vol. XXIV, *Zwingli and Bullinger*, ed. G.W. Bromiley, pp. 254–6.)

DOCUMENT V, iii   Martin Bucer to Brentius

Martin Bucer came to England at the invitation of Cranmer in 1548, and was given a teaching post in Cambridge. He was very critical of the negative tone of the English Reformation, and of its lack of evangelical content.

Dated at Cambridge, 15 May 1550

Affairs in this country are in a very feeble state: the people are in want of teachers. Things are for the most part carried on by the means of ordinances, which the majority obey very grudgingly, and by the removal of the instruments of the ancient superstition: and some persons have been, and still continue to be, very docile pupils of our countrymen, with carnal liberty and spiritual bondage. The king, however, is godly and learned to a miracle: he is well acquainted with Latin, and has a fair knowledge of Greek; he speaks Italian, and is learning French. He is now studying moral philosophy from Cicero and Aristotle: but no study delights him more than that of the holy scriptures, of which he daily reads about ten chapters with the greatest attention. Some youths from among the principal nobility follow his example in these studies, and with good success. Of those devoted to the service of religion but a very small number have as yet entirely addicted themselves to the kingdom of Christ. In the universities the Balthazars[1] for the most part have the direction of affairs; though there are not wanting very many, even among the heads, who are sound in godliness and well instructed to the kingdom of God.

It is a very great alleviation of my anxiety, that I am permitted to set forth the kingdom of Christ with the most entire freedom, in my lectures, disputations, and Latin sermons. But ever since August it has pleased God to chasten me by severe illness, the remains of which still confine me, namely, excessive weakness in my legs, arms and hands. In my left hand one, and in my right hand two fingers, still refuse their office; so that I am not yet able to write.[2]

> (*Original Letters relative to the Reformation in England*, ed. H. Robinson (Parker Society, 1847), II, 542–3.)

1. Men given to feasting, i.e. idle worldlings.
2. Martin Bucer died on 28 February 1551.

DOCUMENT V, iv   Calvin on the sovereignty of God — from the *Sermons on Deuteronomy*, 1555

By 1570 the main theological influence on the English Reformation came from John Calvin, who died in 1565. The logic of his doctrine was more rigorous than that of either Luther or Bucer, concentrating particularly upon the predestination of the Elect to salvation.

Observe in connection with the deliverance of the Israelites that the main point is not that God should save us from the hands of our enemies and keep us longer in this world. What good were all that, if God were not gracious to us and if we did not call upon Him and commit ourselves to Him? There is no point in our staying here three days and a half, for what is this life if not a feeble shadow which passes soon away? The point is rather that we should recognize God as our eternal Saviour, that we so walk in His fear that we may expect from Him not only guidance for a brief moment but that in the end He should take us to Himself, that after this pilgrimage we may enjoy an inheritance laid up for us in heaven. The blessings of this life are to be used only for our salvation, otherwise they become a curse and those on whom God has conferred the most are the most blameworthy in His eyes, for we corrupt all the graces of God when we are not incited by them to render Him homage, placing ourselves completely in His hands as our refuge. Let us then not be as the brute beasts grubbing in the earth, but let us lift our eyes to the heavens and recognize that He calls us to Himself and that toward Him we move till we be conjoined with Him forever.

(From *Calvini Opera*, Corpus Reformatorum XXXV [selected English text from *The Age of the Reformation*, ed. R.H. Bainton, pp. 132–4].)

Select Bibliography

(The place of publication, unless otherwise stated, is London.)

SECTION A: SOURCES

1. Gilbert Burnet, *History of the Reformation of the Church of England*, ed. Nicholas Pocock (1865). A work originally written between 1679 and 1715, containing careful transcripts of many original documents.

2. A.G. Dickens and Dorothy Carr (eds.), *The Reformation in England to the Accession of Elizabeth* (1967). A handy modern collection with useful commentary.

3. G.R. Elton, *The Tudor Constitution* (2nd ed., Cambridge, 1982). Sections 7 and 9 relate to the Church.

4. John Foxe, *Acts and Monuments of the English Martyrs*, ed. S.R. Cattley and G. Townsend (1837–41). The best edition; contains transcripts of many proceedings relating to the trials of protestants under Mary.

5. W.H. Frere and W.M. Kennedy (eds.), *Visitation Articles and Injunctions* (1910). Formal documents relating to the administration of the Church, some in Latin. Useful, but heavy-going for the non-specialist.

6. H. Gee and W.J. Hardy (eds.), *Documents Illustrative of English Church History* (1896). An old-fashioned 'constitutional' collection, but useful.

7. P.L. Hughes and J.F. Larkin (eds.), *Tudor Royal Proclamations* (New Haven, 1964, 1968). Religious edicts scattered about in a chronologically arranged sequence. Modern and readable format.

8. Hastings Robinson (ed.), *Original Letters Relating to the Reformation*

(1846). Two volumes of letters which passed between the English reformers and their Continental friends, translated into English.

9. T. Rymer (ed.), *Foedera, conventiones . . . et acta publica* (1704–32). Valuable collection of formal documents. Not for the faint-hearted.

10. A. Luders *et al.* (ed.), *Statutes of the Realm* (1810–28). Contains the complete text of every statute. It is sometimes enlightening to get beyond the familiar extracts.

11. J. Strype, *Ecclesiastical Memorials* (1820). An early eighteenth-century work, published originally in 1720. Like Burnet, useful for its original documents, many of which have since been destroyed.

12. C.H. Williams, *English Historical Documents, 1485–1558* (1967). Part V deals with the Church; a wide-ranging collection, with modern commentary.

SECTION B: SECONDARY WORKS

I. General

13. P. Collinson, *The Religion of Protestants* (Oxford, 1983). Discusses the distinguishing features of the reformed faith.

14. C. Cross, *Church and People, 1450–1660* (1976). Better on the dissenting movements than on the Church itself; a good general survey.

15. A.G. Dickens, *The English Reformation* (2nd Edition, 1990). The classic 'Anglican' exposition.

16. A.G. Dickens, *Reformation Essays* (1982). A collection of twenty-eight papers written over more than thirty years. Some are extremely useful, but the collection should be used selectively.

17. C. Haigh, *The English Reformation Revised* (1987). A collection of eleven essays, five of them by Haigh, arguing the case for the continuity of the English Church, and denying that the Reformation had strong popular roots.

18. Philip Hughes, *The Reformation in England* (1950–4). The classic 'catholic' exposition; very learned, but rather heavy-going.

19. P. Lake and M. Dowling (eds.), *Protestantism and the National Church in the Sixteenth Century* (1987). A useful but miscellaneous collection, many of the essays by younger scholars. Some refreshing new perspectives.

20. D. Loades, *Politics, Censorship and the English Reformation* (1991). A collection of essays written over twenty-five years; one or two new.

21. T.M. Parker, *The English Reformation to 1558* (1950). A useful short introduction, but now distinctly dated.

22. J.J. Scarisbrick, *The Reformation and the English People* (Oxford, 1984). Ford lectures, uneven in quality. Presenting the same general thesis as Haigh.

II. Historiography

23. C. Haigh, 'The recent historiography of the English Reformation', in *The English Reformation Revised*, 19–31 (see Bib. 17).

24. R. O'Day, *The Debate on the English Reformation* (1986). A good backward look, but a bit premature in terms of the latest controversy.

III. The Royal Supremacy

25. C. Cross, *The Royal Supremacy in the Elizabethan Church* (1969). A good and manageable discussion, with documents.

26. G.R. Elton, *Policy and Police* (Cambridge, 1972). Ford lectures; a very thorough and penetrating examination of the way in which the Henrician Reformation was enforced. Invaluable for an understanding of Tudor society.

27. J. Guy, *Tudor England* (Oxford, 1988). The most up-to-date and comprehensive textbook treatment. A good starting-point.

28. Norman Jones, *Faith by Statute* (1982). Effective critique of J.E. Neale's interpretation of the 1559 Parliament. Believes that Elizabeth wanted a full protestant settlement from the start.

29. D. Loades, *The Oxford Martyrs* (1970). Rather wider than its title implies. Looks at the theoretical and practical implications of the supremacy between 1535 and 1558.

30. D. Loades, *The Reign of Mary Tudor* (2nd ed., 1991). A history of the reign which examines the implications of the reconciliation with Rome.

31. G.R. Redworth, *In Defence of the Church Catholic* (Oxford, 1990). A biography of Stephen Gardiner, examining his relationship with the supremacy.

32. J.J. Scarisbrick, *Henry VIII* (1968). Still the best general history of the reign; rather heavy-going on canon law.

IV. The Pre-Reformation Church

33. M. Aston, 'Lollardy and the Reformation; survival or revival', *History*, 49 (1964). Argues the importance of Lollardy for Reformation 'footholds'.

34. M. Aston, *England's Iconoclasts* (Oxford, 1989). Deals comprehensively with the role of images and their destruction in the shaping of the Anglican tradition. Learned and packed with information.

35. M. Bowker, *The Secular Clergy in the Diocese of Lincoln, 1495–1520* (Cambridge, 1968). An outstanding study of the largest diocese in England.

36. Peter Heath, *The English Parish Clergy on the Eve of the Reformation* (1969). The best general discussion of the late medieval clergy as a professional group.

37. Anne Hudson, *Lollards and their Books* (1985). The connections between literacy and dissent in the late fifteenth and early sixteenth century. Supports older interpretations of the Reformation.

38. D. Knowles, *The Religious Orders in England*, Vol. III (Cambridge, 1961). Still the best analysis of the state of the monasteries just before their dissolution. Judicious and informative.

39. H. Maynard Smith, *Pre-Reformation England* (1938). Still a useful survey, though out-of-date in some of its interpretations.

40. J.A.F. Thomson, *The Later Lollards, 1414–1520* (Oxford, 1965). A valuable account of the attitude of the Church to dissent on the eve of the Reformation.

41. J.A.F. Thomson, *The Transformation of Medieval England, 1370–1529* (1984). A textbook which usefully crosses traditional chronological boundaries to set the Church in its political and social context.

V. Humanism

42. M. Dowling, *Humanism in the Age of Henry VIII* (1986). A useful updating of McConica (Bib. 48); good on the court, and on education.

43. M. Dowling, 'Gospel and the Court; reformation under Henry VIII' in *Protestantism and the National Church* (Bib. 19). Distinguishes usefully between protestants and reformers; cuts Catherine Parr down to size.

44. E. Duffy and B. Bradshaw (eds.), *Humanism, Reform and Reformation* (Cambridge, 1989). A collection of essays on the career of John Fisher, Bishop of Rochester. The best treatment of the subject; excellent on the meaning of 'reform'.

45. G.R. Elton, *Reform and Renewal* (Cambridge, 1973). The Wiles Lectures. Presents Thomas Cromwell as an idealist and intellectual; original and convincing.

46. A. Fox, *Thomas More* (Oxford, 1982). An intellectual biography; the best study of More's thought.

47. J. Guy and A. Fox, *Reassessing the Henrician Age* (Oxford, 1986). Intelligent and polite critique of Elton's *Tudor Revolution in Government*, but also advancing new ideas on the intellectual context of reform.

48. J.K. McConica, *English Humanism and Reformation Politics* (Oxford, 1965). A rather exaggerated assessment of the importance of 'Erasmianism' in Henrician politics.

49. J. Simon, *Education and Society in Tudor England* (1966). The standard treatment of the subject; necessary background to any study of the literature of the Reformation.

VI. The Henrician Reformation

50. Margaret Bowker, *The Henrician Reformation: The Diocese of*

Lincoln under John Longland, 1521–1547 (Cambridge, 1981). An excellent case study, although the 'case' is rather a large one.

51. Susan Brigden, *London and the Reformation* (Oxford, 1989). Important; packed with information and anecdote. The problem is to see the wood for the trees.

52. W.A. Clebsch, *England's Earliest Protestants, 1520–1535* (New Haven, 1964). An examination of the first Continental influences, mainly on Cambridge graduates. Valuable.

53. D. Knowles, *The Religious Orders in England* (see Bib. 38). The best account of the dissolution.

54. S. Lehmberg, *The Reformation Parliament, 1529–1536* (Cambridge, 1970). A political analysis of how the parliamentary campaign was managed.

55. G.R. Redworth, 'A study in the formulation of policy; the genesis and evolution of the Act of Six Articles', *Journal of Ecclesiastical History*, 37 (1986). A recent 'anatomy' of the Henrician reaction; enlightening.

56. L.B. Smith, 'Henry VIII and the protestant triumph', *American Historical Review*, 71 (1966). The power struggle in the last weeks of Henry VIII's life, which explains the Edwardian Reformation.

57. Joyce Youings, *The Dissolution of the Monasteries* (1972). A useful, short documents-and-commentary exercise. Not as academic as Bib. 53; from a research base in the West Country.

VII. The Edwardian Reformation

58. M.L. Bush, *The Government Policy of Protector Somerset* (1975). Demolishes the traditional image of the 'good duke', and puts his religious policy in context.

59. D.E. Hoak, *The King's Council in the Reign of Edward VI* (Cambridge, 1976). The best study of the politics of the reign. Examines the role of religion in factional conflict.

60. D.E. Hoak, 'Rehabilitating the Duke of Northumberland; politics and political control, 1549–1553', in J. Loach and R. Tittler (eds.), *The Mid-Tudor Polity, 1540–1560* (1980). Why did the duke opt for radical protestantism?

61. W.K. Jordan, *Edward VI: The Young King* (1968). Narrative history of Somerset's Protectorate, 1547–9. Useful, but interpretations should be treated with care.

62. W.K. Jordan, *Edward VI: The Threshold of Power* (1970). Covers Northumberland's years in power (1549–53). Argues that the young king was increasingly in command. Unconvincing.

63. A. Kreider, *English Chantries: The Road to Dissolution* (Cambridge, Mass., 1979). The only satisfactory study of an important subject.

64. Andrew Pettegree, *Foreign Protestant Communities in Sixteenth-Century London* (Oxford, 1986). Particularly good on the formally established congregations of Edward's reign, and their relations with the English Church.

65. J.B. Phillips, *The Reformation of Images: The Destruction of Art in England, 1525–1660* (1973). Should be read in conjunction with Bib. 34. Good on the iconoclastic policies of Edward's governments.

VIII. The Marian Reaction

66. Dermot Fenlon, *Heresy and Obedience in Tridentine Italy* (Cambridge, 1972). A study of Cardinal Reginald Pole in Italy and in England. Invaluable for an understanding of his attitude and policy.

67. J. Loach, 'The Marian establishment and the printing press', *English Historical Review*, 101 (1986). Argues that the Marian Church was successfully pursuing its own priorities.

68. D. Loades, *The Reign of Mary Tudor* (2nd ed., 1991). The only full history of the reign. Should be read in conjunction with Bib. 29.

69. J.A. Muller, *Stephen Gardiner and the Tudor Reaction* (Cambridge, 1926). Well documented and still useful, but should be read in conjunction with Bib. 31.

70. R.H. Pogson, 'Revival and reform in Mary Tudor's Church: a question of money', *Journal of Ecclesiastical History*, 25 (1974). Argues that the Marian Church did a good job in adverse circumstances; convincing.

71. R.H. Pogson, 'Reginald Pole and the priorities of government in Mary Tudor's church', *Historical Journal*, 18 (1975). Useful; should be read in conjunction with Bib. 66.

72. R. Tittler, *The Reign of Mary I* (1983). A 'Seminar' study; very brief but the best introduction.

IX. The Elizabethan Settlement

73. P. Collinson, *The Elizabethan Puritan Movement* (1967). The classic study, never superseded. Demonstrates that puritanism was not dissent.

74. P. Collinson, *Godly People* (1983). A collection of essays on Elizabethan protestants, written over a number of years. Full of interesting material.

75. P. Collinson, *Archbishop Grindal: The Struggle for a Reformed Church* (1980). An excellent biography of Elizabeth's least favoured archbishop.

76. C. Haigh, 'From monopoly to minority: catholicism in early modern England', *Transactions of the Royal Historical Society*, 5th series, 31 (1981). Argues that the catholic rearguard action was prolonged, and was eventually betrayed by its own leaders. A very important 'revisionist' essay.

77. W.P. Haugaard, *Elizabeth and the English Reformation* (1968). Useful factual account, now somewhat out of date.

78. W.S. Hudson, *The Cambridge Connection and the Elizabethan Settlement of 1559* (Durham, N.C., 1980). Intellectual origins and associations of the architects of the settlement.

79. Norman Jones, *Faith by Statute* (see Bib. 28).

80. P. Lake, *Moderate Puritans and the Elizabethan Church* (1982). A study of the mainstream of Elizabethan religious thought. Probably the best study of the Church as such during the period.

81. W. MacCaffrey, *The Shaping of the Elizabethan Regime* (1969). Puts the religious settlement into its political context.

82. P. McGrath, *Papists and Puritans under Elizabeth I* (1967). The best general account of catholic recusancy. Less good on the puritans.

83. V.N. Olsen, *John Foxe and the Elizabethan Church* (Berkeley, 1973). The best analysis of Foxe and his influence to date.

X. Special and Local Studies

84. P. Clark, *English Provincial Society from the Reformation to the Revolution: Religion, Politics and Society in Kent, 1500–1640* (Brighton, 1977). Contains a valuable examination of the Reformation in an important county from the viewpoint of a social historian.

85. G.J. Cuming, *A History of the Anglican Liturgy* (1969). A manageable treatment of a large and complex subject.

86. J.F. Davis, *Heresy and Reformation in South-East England* (1983).

87. A.G. Dickens, *Lollards and Protestants in the Diocese of York* (Oxford, 1959). The best regional study of the origins of the Reformation.

88. C.W. Dugmore, *The Mass and the English Reformers* (1958). Out of date, but still useful because it has not been superseded by any comparable work.

89. K. Firth, *The Apocalyptic Tradition in Reformation Britain, 1530–1645* (Oxford, 1979). The best general treatment of one of the main strands of religious radicalism.

90. C. Haigh, *Reformation and Resistance in Tudor Lancashire* (Manchester, 1975). A seminal study of the most conservative of all the English counties. Argues that protestantism made little impression outside the larger towns.

91. F. Heal, *Of Prelates and Princes* (1980). The social and political role of the episcopate.

92. R. Houlbrooke, *Church Courts and the People during the English Reformation* (Oxford, 1979). The best general study of the formal influence of the Church on the lives of ordinary people.

93. J. N. King, *English Reformation Literature,* (Princeton, 1982). The best survey of the reformers' use of printed polemic.

94. S.E. Lehmberg, *The Reformation of Cathedrals* (Princeton, 1988). Uneven, but the only treatment of an important subject. Good on music.

95. D. Loades, *Thomas Cranmer* (Bangor, 1991). A brief introduction.

96. Diarmaid MacCulloch, *Suffolk and the Tudors* (Cambridge, 1987). An outstanding local study.

97. J.W. Martin, *The Religious Radicals in Tudor England* (Oxford, 1989). A collection of essays; uneven, but containing some very useful insights.

98. R. O'Day and F. Heal, *Continuity and Change: Personnel and Administration of the Church of England, 1500–1642* (1976). The best study of the clergy as a professional group during the Reformation.

99. J.E. Oxley, *The Reformation in Essex to the Death of Mary* (1965). A useful study of one of the earliest centres of protestant influence.

100. J. Ridley, *Thomas Cranmer* (1962). The best biography so far; important.

101. R. Whiting, *The Blind Faith of the People* (Cambridge, 1988). A study of the diocese of Exeter. Demonstrates conclusively that the majority of Englishmen simply did what they were told. Valuable.

102. Glanmor Williams, *Welsh Reformation Essays* (Cardiff, 1967). The best work dealing specifically with Wales.

103. Glanmor Williams, *The Reformation in Wales* (Bangor, 1991). A new short account; valuable.

104. C.H. Williams, *William Tyndale* (1969). The standard life.

Index